I0566944

Our Favorite Tested & Tried Recipes

Cooking With The Richardson's

LaRose Angela Richardson & Dr. Richard C. Richardson

REJOICE
Essential Publishing

LaRose Angela Richardson & Dr. Richard C. Richardson/Rejoice Essential Publishing

PO BOX 512

Effingham, SC 29541

www.republishing.org

Our Favorite Tested & Tried Recipes Cooking With The Richardson's/LaRose Angela Richardson & Dr. Richard C. Richardson

ISBN-13: 978-1-956775-55-6

COOKING WITH THE RICHARDSON'S

John 6:35 says, "Then Jesus declared, "I am the Bread of Life. Whoever comes to me will never go hungry, and whoever believes in me will never be thirsty."

Baked Oxtails With Gravy

Barbecue Brunswick Stew

Loaded Mashed Potatoes

Juicy Seafood Dressing

Old Fashioned Jelly Cake

Can't Wait To Eat The Last Piece

Key Lime Cake

Tasty Boil Peanuts

Flavorful Dishes To Cook For Your Families That Will Have Them Coming Back For More!!

INTRODUCTION

I would like to thank God for giving my husband and me the motivation and encouragement to write this cookbook to express our love for cooking for our family. Also, for the life-changing scriptures that are added to each recipe. The cook will get the Word of God for their spirit and the recipe for food for their body in the natural. For everyone who loves to cook and try new recipes that will be the hit of any dinner party or cookout, all these recipes are tasty and cost-efficient, and you can stay within your budget each week. Plus, there will be plenty of leftovers for the next day. These are my favorite recipes that I have cooked over the years and I critiqued them to my taste, so as you cook these dishes, you will grow in faith as well.

ACKNOWLEDGMENTS

I would like to dedicate this book to my mom, Lynette Roberson, who departed this world on April 28, 2008. My mom loved to cook and taught me how to cook many dishes and critique them to my taste palate. Here are some recipes she taught me to cook and some of my own that I picked up over the years. I have experimented with other ingredients to see which ones would go great with certain dishes and enhance the flavor of the dishes. I tested and tried all these recipes when I first got married 13 years ago and I have continued to cook them regularly.

I pray that you will get inspired as you cook, read, and meditate on the scripture as you receive food for your body and your soul. Come on. Let's wake up our taste buds and our spirits with the Word of God.

SCRIPTURES

Genesis 1:29 (AMP) says, "So God said, "Behold, I have given you every plant yielding seed that is on the surface of the entire earth, and every tree which has fruit yielding seed; it shall be food for you;""

Matthew 6:25 (AMP) says, "Therefore I tell you, stop being worried or anxious (perpetually, uneasy, distracted) about your life, as to what you will eat or what you will drink; nor about your body, as to what you will wear. Is life not more than food, and the body more than clothing."

PRAYER

Father God, in the name of Jesus, we pray for everyone that has purchased this cookbook in Jesus's name. Lord, allow them to feel your presence stronger than ever before in Jesus's name. Allow them to be guided by your Spirit as they read these scriptures for each recipe in Jesus's name. Lord, whatever they need, You said that You would supply their every need, such as Your riches in glory by Christ Jesus. Lord, help them to always have food in their refrigerator, cabinets, and pantry and always have an overabundance of everything that they need in their homes in Jesus's name. I decree and declare that their house will never be in lack in Jesus's name. Lord, help them to always have more than enough to take care of their household in Jesus's name. Lord, help them to understand that they need to have a closer relationship with you from this day forward in Jesus's name. I decree and declare that they will have peace in their homes and lives in Jesus's name. I decree and declare that whatever they put their hand to do will be prosperous and successful in Jesus's name. Lord, we give You all the glory, honor, and praise for the changes that have already begun in their lives from reading this prayer and using the recipes in this cookbook in Jesus's name. Amen.

Table of Contents

Table of Contents

Baked Macaroni And Cheese

Psalm 119:11 (AMP) says, "Your word I have treasured and stored in my heart, That I may not sin against You."

6-8 people   45"   Easy

---

2 ½ cups of uncooked macaroni
2 ½ tbsp of flour

1 ¼ tsp of salt
1 tsp of pepper
4 Tbsp of margarine

3 cups of shredded cheddar cheese
1 cup of milk

---

1. Preheat the oven to 350 degrees.

2. Cook pasta until tender, drain, mix all dry ingredients together, and set aside.

3. Spray oven safe bowl or dish with cooking spray. Place half of the macaroni inside the dish.

4. Sprinkle half of the flour mixture over the top, cut the margarine into small slices, and put half of the margarine on top of the flour.

5. Sprinkle 1 ½ of the shredded cheese over the butter and re-peat the steps until the bowl is full.

6. Pour the milk over the top of the mixture.

7. Cover with foil and bake at 350 degrees for 35 minutes. Remove the foil and bake for an additional 10 minutes.

8. Serve hot.

Barbecue Macaroni And Cheese

Psalm 118:14 (AMP) says, "The LORD is my strength and song, And He has become my salvation."

6 - 8 people   45"   Easy

---

1 pkg of Kraft Deluxe Macaroni & Cheese Dinner

½ lb. of lean ground beef

½ cup of finely chopped onions

2 Tbsp of garlic powder

½ Bull's Eye Memphis Style

Barbecue Sauce (or substitute)

2 slices of Oscar Mayer Bacon cooked, crumbled

---

1. Preheat the oven to 300 degrees.

2. Cook the macaroni as directed on the package. Meanwhile, brown meat with onions and garlic in a large skillet and drain.

3. Add macaroni, cheese sauce, and barbecue sauce to the meat mixture in the skillet. Stir. Cook for 2 to 3 minutes or until heated through. Stirring occasionally.

4. Place in the oven at 300 degrees for 25 minutes with shredded cheese on top.

5. Top with bacon and serve.

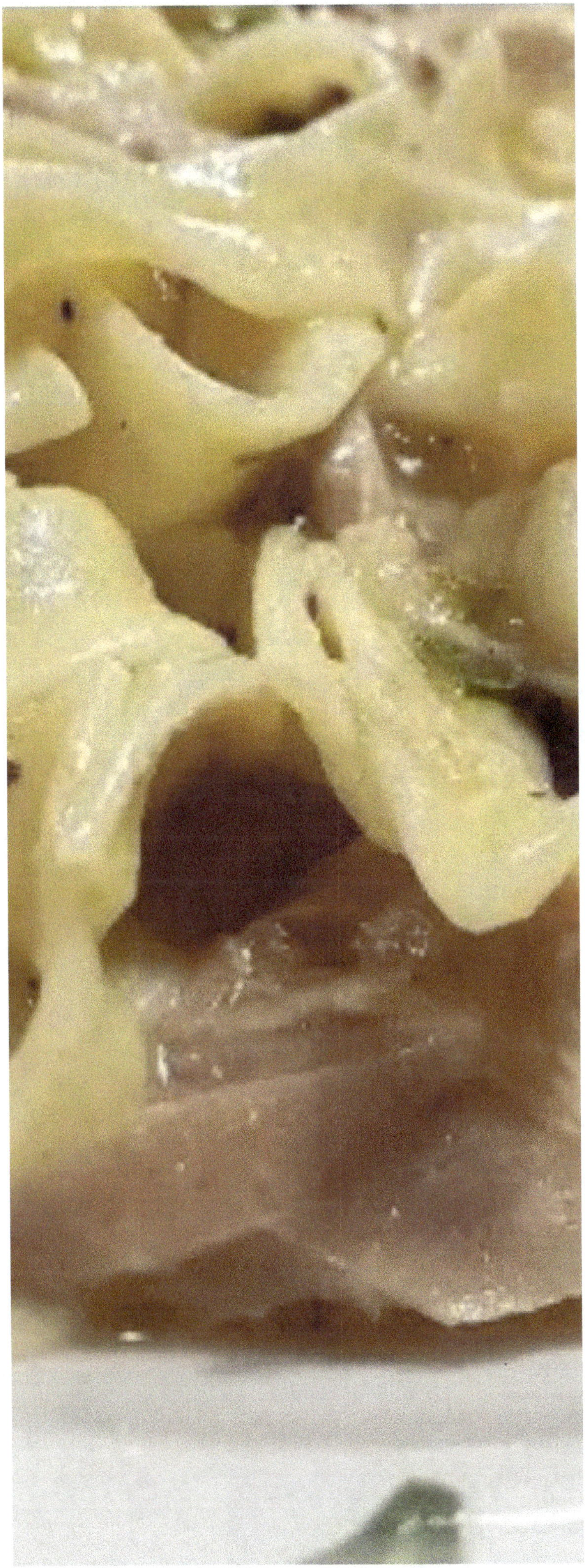

Seasoned Egg Noodles

2 1/2 cups of chicken or beef broth
1/2 pkg of Egg Noodles
1 tsp of soul food seasoning
1 tsp of Old Bay seasoning.

6 - 8 people   35"   Easy

Acts 1:8 (AMP) says, "But you shall receive power and ability when the Holy Spirit comes upon you; and you will be My witnesses (to tell people about Me) both in Jerusalem and in all Judea, and Samaria, and even to the ends of the earth."

1. Put chicken broth in a 6 qt saucepan and bring to a boil. Add all seasoning before putting noodles into boiling water.

2. Place 1/2 package of egg noodles in the broth and cook until done. Let the noodles sit for 20 minutes to finish cooking and soak up some of the broth into the noodles.

3. Let it cool, then eat it with other meat dishes.

Pasta Salad with Crab and Shrimp

6 - 8 people   40"   Easy

---

1 lb. pasta spaghetti
1 cucumber peeled and cut into small pieces
3 tomatoes cut into small pieces
1 bottle of Zesty Italian dressing
1 lb. of cooked shrimp
1 pkg of flake crab cut into small pieces
1 pkg of shredded sharp cheddar cheese

Acts 3:2 (AMP) says, "And a man who had been unable to walk from birth was being carried along, whom they used to set down every day at the gate of the temple, which is called Beautiful, so that he could beg alms from those entering the temple."

1. Cook spaghetti as directed on the package and drain.

2. In a bowl, put spaghetti, cucumber, and tomatoes. Stir until blended well.

3. Add shrimp, flake crab, and a bottle of Zesty Italian until all of it is mixed together.

4. Refrigerate for 30 minutes. Serve and add shredded cheese on top of it.

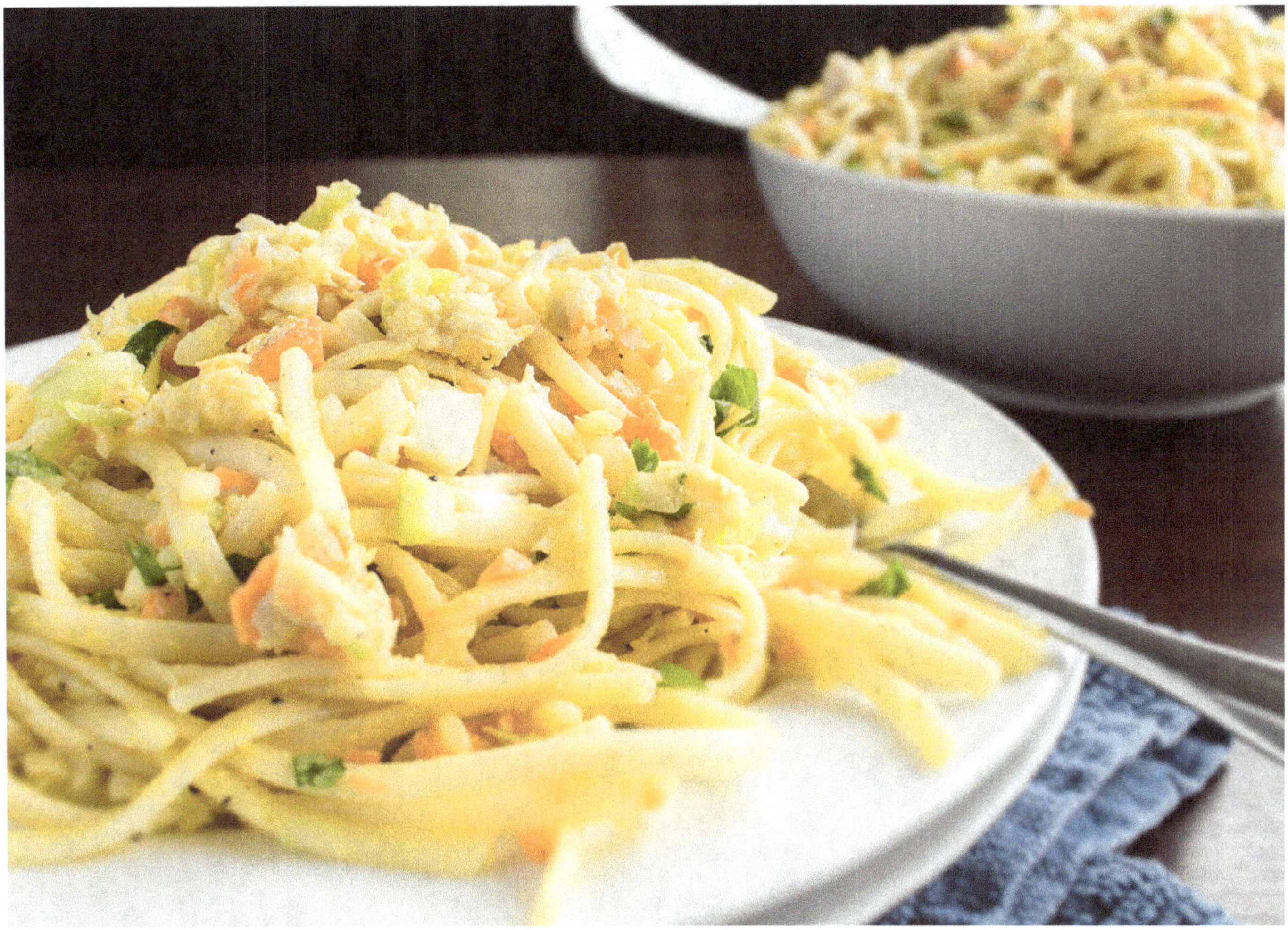

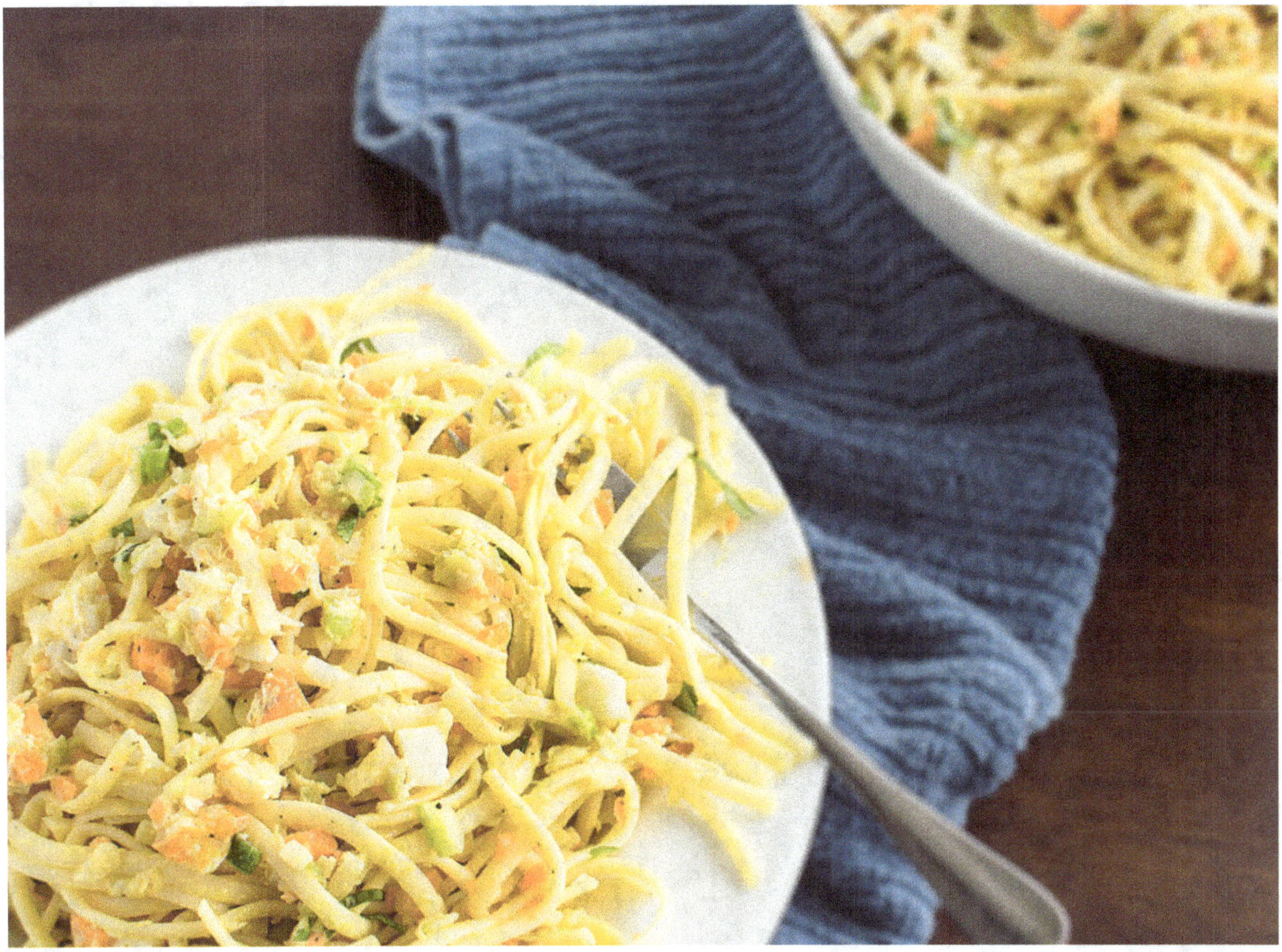

Baked Spaghetti

Acts 3:6 (AMP) says, "But Peter said, "Silver and gold I do not have; but what I do have I give to you: In the name (authority, power) of Jesus Christ of Nazarene---(begin now to) walk and go on walking!"

6 - 8 people   50"   Easy

---

1 lb. hamburger meat
1 lb. spaghetti
1 jar of spaghetti sauce

3 tbsp of grape jelly
1 pkg Goya Ham flavored concentrate

1 cup of shredded cheddar cheese

---

1. Cook hamburger meat until it is brown on medium heat. Pour off excess grease.

2. Mix spaghetti sauce with the hamburger meat heat until it comes to a boil, then turn down the heat to simmer.

3. Put 3 tablespoons of grape jelly in the mixture and let it melt into the mixture. Add 1 pkg of Goya Ham flavored concentrate into the mixture.

4. Cook for 10 minutes on simmer so flavors can mix together while you are cooking the spaghetti. Cook spaghetti as directed on the package until done.

5. Sprinkle cheese on top of spaghetti before serving.

Shrimp Fettuccine Alfredo

Acts 3:26 (AMP) says, "It was for you first of all that God raised up His Servant and Son (Jesus) and sent Him to bless you by turning every one of you from wicked ways."

4- 5 people   35"   Easy

---

8 oz. cream cheese   ½ cup of butter   1 lb. shrimped, cooked
¾ cup of parmesan cheese,   ½ cup of milk   1 tsp Soul food seasoning
grated   1 box of fettuccine   1 tsp Old Bay seasoning

---

1. Cook and drain fettuccine.

2. Cut cream cheese into small pieces.

3. In a large saucepan, combine cream cheese, parmesan cheese, butter, and milk. Stir constantly until smooth.

4. Toss pasta lightly with sauce, coating well. Add seasoning and shrimp and stir again to coat the shrimp with the mixture.

5. Serve warm

Steamed Cabbage with Smoked Sausages

Psalm 107:20 (AMP) says, "He sent His word and healed them And rescued them from their destruction."

6-8 people   60"   Easy

1 large head of cabbage chopped up
1 lb. smoked sausages chopped up
1 onion diced up or min-ced onion
½ stick of butter or margarine
4 cups of water
6 chicken bouillon cubes
2 tbsp of Cajun seasoning
1 tbsp of dried parsley
Salt and pepper to taste

1. Add all ingredients except salt and pepper to taste in the crock pot or stock pot. Set on medium heat and cook until cabbage reaches desired tenderness.

2. Salt and pepper to taste. Serve with juices and cornbread.

This recipe is easy and delicious.

Chili

10 - 12 people	60"	Easy

---

1 lb. Hamburger meat cooked and drained

2 pkg of chili mix, mild

2 cans of kidney beans

2 cans of chopped tomatoes

2 tbsp of Old Bay seasoning

2 tbsp of soul food seasoning

1 large jar of spaghetti sauce, any flavor

1 pkg of shredded cheddar cheese

---

1. Brown hamburger meat on high heat in a stock pot on top of the stove and drain excess oil.

2. Pour hamburger meat into the crock pot, then add chili mix and mix until blended together.

3. Add kidney beans undrained, tomatoes, and spaghetti sauce. Stir everything until it is mixed together.

4. Add old bay seasoning and soul food seasoning. Stir and mix them together in the crock pot.

5. Let it come to a boil in a crock pot on high heat, then turn it down to low and let it simmer for 45 minutes, occasionally stirring to prevent sticking.

6. Let cool and serve with shredded cheese or crackers on top.

Barbecue Brunswick Stew

1 lb. pork roast cut up into small pieces (already cooked)
1 med. onion cut into small pieces
4 celery stalks cut into small pieces
2 tsp of garlic seasoning
2 tsp of soul food seasoning
4 cups of water
10 chicken bouillon cubes, crushed
1 bottle of barbecue sauce, original
2 cups of peeled potatoes and chopped
1 can of green lima beans
1 can of cream corn
1 can of whole kernel corn
1 can of tomatoes and okra
1 large jar of spaghetti sauce, any flavor
¼ cup of Worcestershire sauce, Heinz

6 - 8 people   100"   Moderate

Psalm 96:1 (AMP) says, "O SING to the LORD a new song; Sing to the LORD. All the earth!"

1. Combine water, bouillon cubes, onion, and celery in a stock pot on medium heat. Cook until celery is translucent.

2. Add pork roast and all the seasonings, lima beans, cream corn, whole kernel corn, tomatoes, and spaghetti sauce. Stir until completely mixed together.

3. Bring mixture to a boil and cook for 30 minutes on medium heat. Stirring occasionally to prevent sticking.

4. Add potatoes and a whole bottle of barbecue sauce to the mixture and cook for 20 more minutes or until the potatoes are done.

5. Let it simmer for 10 more minutes on low heat.

6. Cool and serve and eat with corn bread or crackers.

Potato Bacon Soup

6 - 8 people   45"   Easy

½ lb. of bacon chopped and crumbled (cooked)	8 bouillon cubes
Bacon drippings from bacon	2 tbsp of flour
4 lg. potatoes, diced	1 tsp of salt
1 medium onion, chopped	½ tsp of sugar
4 cups of water	1 tsp of Old Bay seasoning
	1 tsp of soul food seasoning

1. Cook bacon and onions in a stock pot on medium heat.

2. After the bacon is cooked, take it out and crumble it up into small pieces. Lay aside.

3. Add water to the stock pot with bacon drippings, seasonings, bouillon cubes, and potatoes. Let it cook until the potatoes are tender and the bouillon cubes have dissolved.

4. Add the remaining ingredients, except bacon, to the mixture and stir it until it is blended together.

5. Cook for 30 minutes, letting it simmer on low heat.

6. The flour will thicken the soup. After the potatoes are done, it is ready.

7. Add crumbled bacon last before serving.

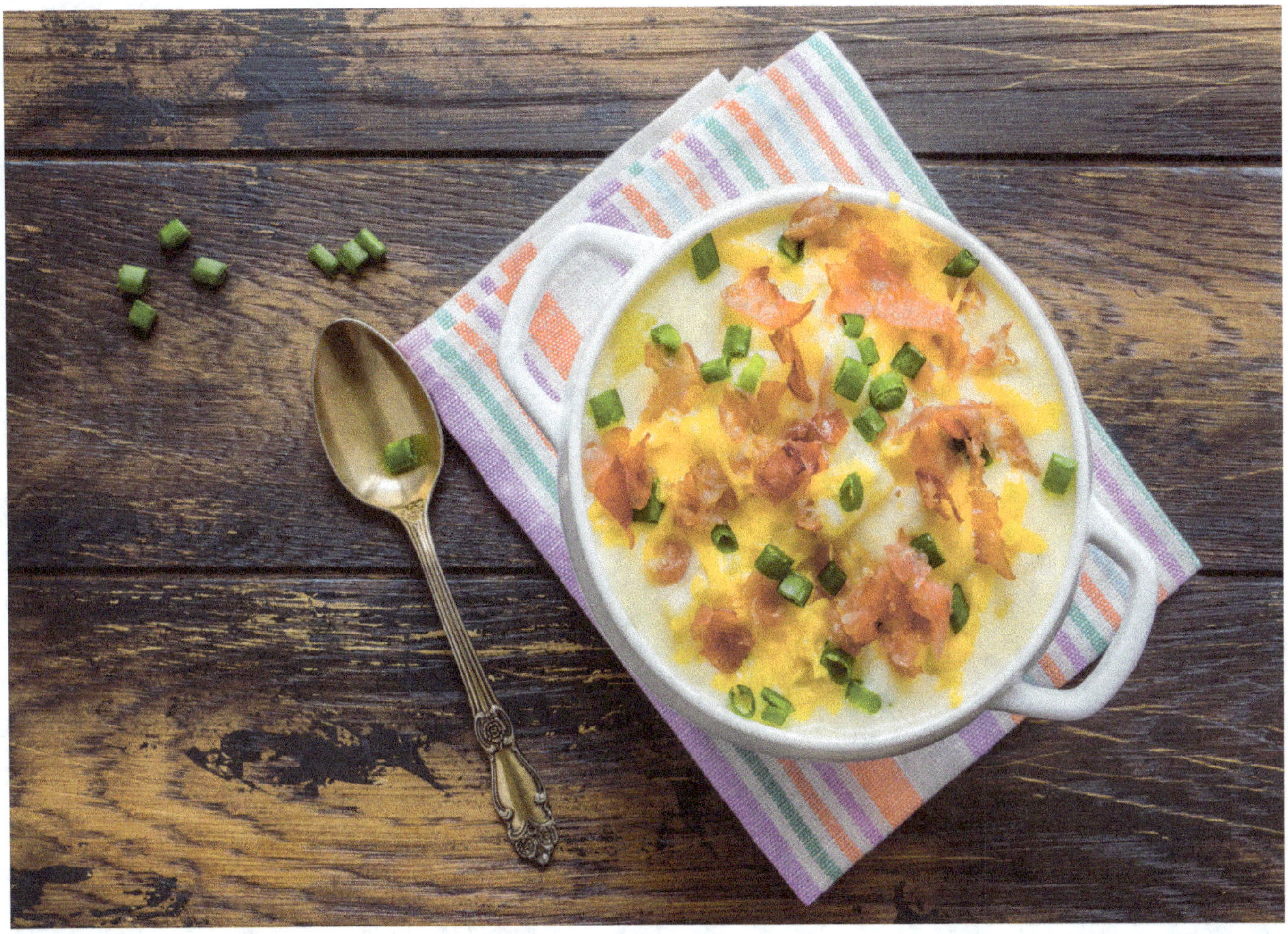

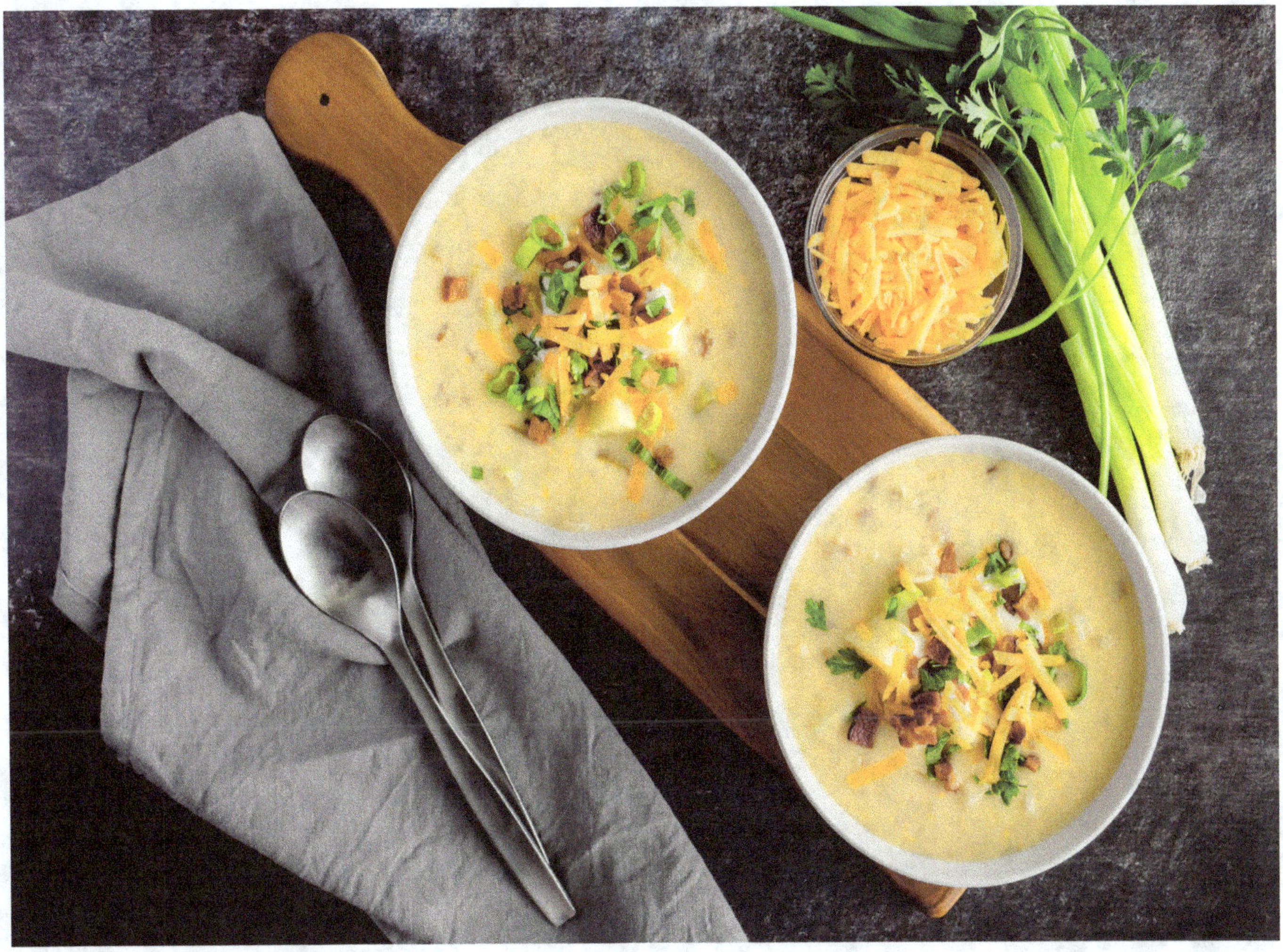

Crab Stew

5 - 7 people   45"   Easy

5 medium potatoes, diced
1 medium onion, diced
1 can cream of mushroom
soup

1 stick of butter
1 can of crab meat
½ gallon of milk
½ tsp parsley

1 tsp of Old Bay seasoning
1 tsp of soul food seasoning
Salt and pepper to taste

1. In a large stock pot, put in potatoes and onions. Boil until potatoes are done.

2. Add all other ingredients and simmer for 30 minutes.

3. Do not boil. Serve with crackers or corn bread.

Homemade Chicken Noodle Soup

8- 10 people   60"   Easy

---

1 rotisserie chicken
1 pkg of egg noodles
2 ½ cups of water

8 chicken bouillon cubes
1 can cream of chicken/
mushroom soup

1 can cream of celery soup
1 can of mixed vegetables

---

1. Take the meat off the bones of the rotisserie chicken and put it aside.

2. Place a medium stock pot on medium heat.

3. Add 2 ½ cups of water, 8 bouillon cubes until the cubes dissolve, and add chicken to the pot.

4. Add soup and mixed vegetables and cook on medium heat for 20 minutes.

5. Add egg noodles to the pot and cook until the egg noodles are done.

6. Turn the heat down to simmer and let it simmer 10 more minutes for the flavors to merge.

7. Serve hot with crackers or a peanut butter and jelly sandwich.

Stew Beef Homemade Soup

6-8 people   60"   Easy

1 lb. of stew beef
1 can of mixed vegetables
1 can of tomatoes
1 small onion, diced
4 medium potatoes, diced

1 tbsp of Old Bay seasoning
1 tbsp of soul food seasoning
3 cups of water

6 beef bouillon cubes
Salt and pepper to taste

1. On medium heat, add water, onion, stew beef, seasonings, and beef bouillon cubes in a large stock pot.

2. Cook until stew beef is done and tender.

3. Add tomatoes, mixed vegetables, and potatoes.

4. Cook until the potatoes are done.

5. Turn the heat down to simmer and simmer for 25 minutes.

6. Serve with rice or crackers.

Stewed Potatoes

Psalm 104:5 (AMP) says, "He established the earth on its foundations. So that it will not be moved forever and ever."

4 - 6 people   50"   Easy

---

4 large potatoes, cubed
3 ½ cups of water
6 chicken bouillon cubes
4 tbsp cornstarch mixed

with water to make a paste
1 tbsp of Old Bay seasoning
1 tbsp of soul food seaso-

ning
1 tbsp of parsley flakes
Salt and pepper to taste

---

1. Cook potatoes in water and bouillon cubes until tender.

2. Add old bay seasoning, soul food seasoning, and parsley seasoning in a pot and stir to mix well.

3. Let simmer for 20 minutes on medium heat.

4. After simmering, bring the mixture back to a boil, add the cornstarch paste mixture to the pot, and stir until it is dissolved.

5. The mixture will begin to thicken up. Put it back on simmer and let simmer for 10 more minutes.

6. Let cool. Serve with a select meat or cornbread.

Homemade Mashed Potatoes

5 large potatoes, diced up
1 stick of butter or margarine
1/3 cup of milk
4 cups of water
½ tsp of salt
Salt and pepper to taste

6 - 8 people   30"   Easy

Psalm 103:1-2 (AMP) says, "BLESS AND affectionately praise the LORD, O my soul, And all that is (deep) within me, bless His holy name."

1. Put 4 cups of water in a stock pot on medium heat.

2. Add salt. Bring to a boil. Cook potatoes until they are tender. Check with a fork to see if the potatoes are cooked. The potatoes should be soft enough to mash with a fork.

3. Drain potatoes with a strainer and put potatoes back into the pot. Add butter.

4. Take a potato masher and mash potatoes until they are smooth. Stir the potatoes and butter until blended.

5. Add milk and stir until well blended together. If you want creamier potatoes, add more milk until you get to desired consistency.

6. Serve with butter or gravy.

Potato Salad

6 - 9 people   30"   Easy

6 potatoes peeled and chopped into cubes
1 jar of Miracle Whip Salad Dressing
6 eggs boiled, peeled, and cut into small pieces

1 jar of sweet salad cubes or sweet relish

1. In a stock pot, cook potatoes until they are tender.

2. Drain potatoes with a strainer and put the potatoes in bowl. Add salad dressing, eggs, and sweet pickles. Mix until smooth.

3. If you want the salad to be creamier, add more salad dressing until it gets to desired consistency.

4. Serve warm or refrigerated and serve chilled.

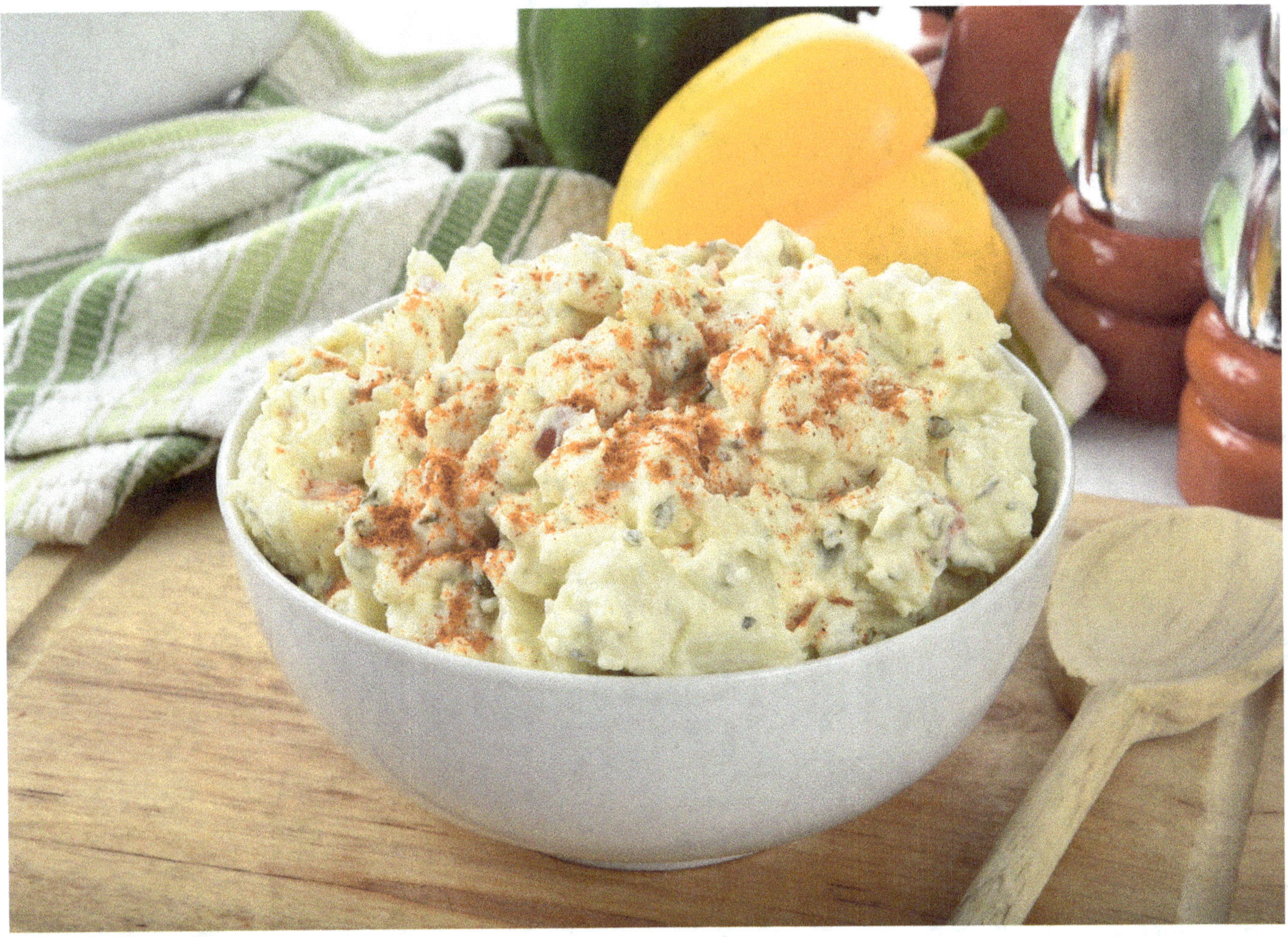

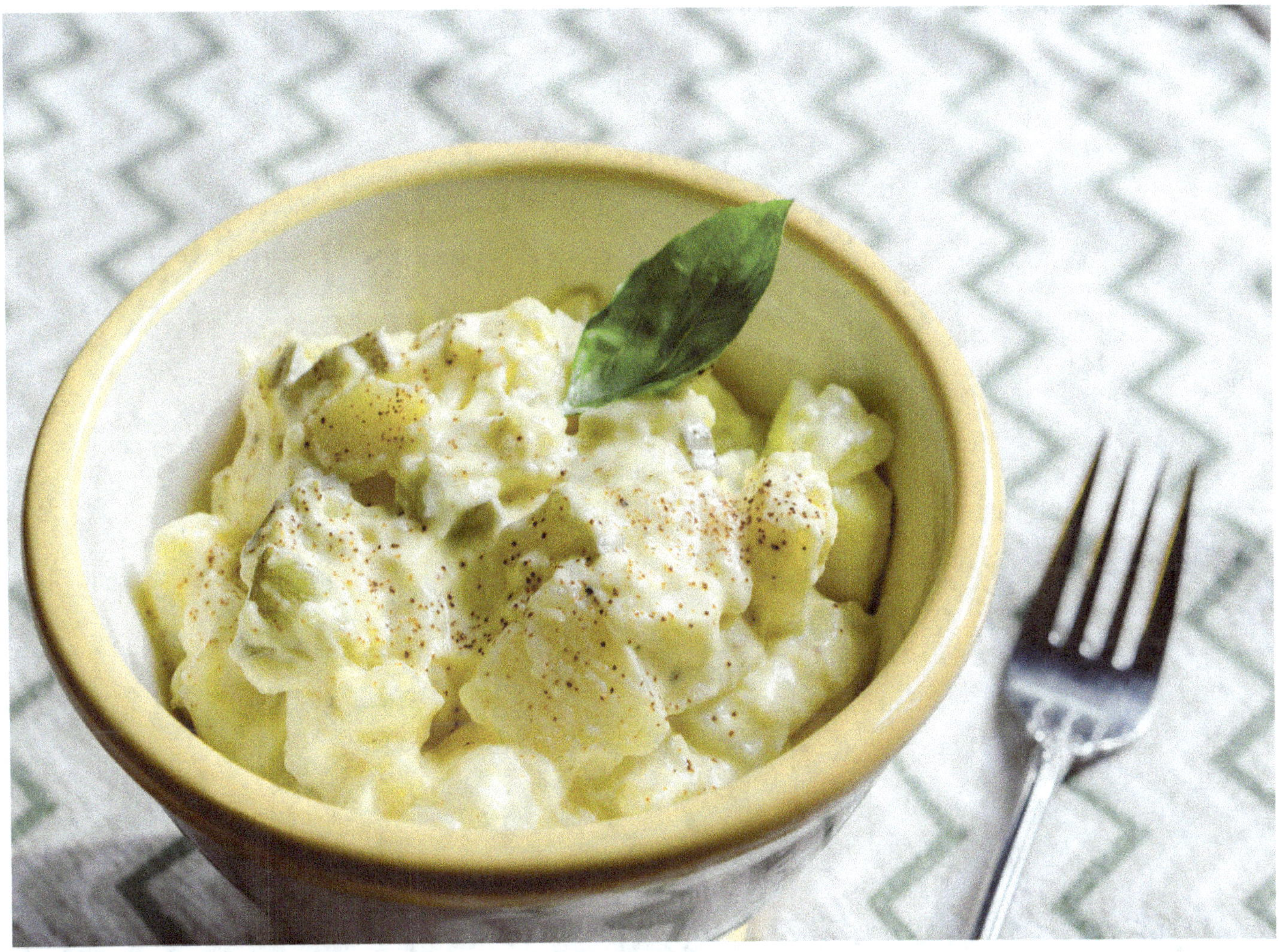

Loaded Baked Potatoes

6 people   60"   Moderate

---

6 baking potatoes	2 tbsp of butter or margarine	1 pkg of bacon bits
Foil to wrap the potatoes	Salt and pepper to taste	Pulled pork
2 tbsp of sour cream		½ cup of barbecue sauce

---

1. Preheat oven to 350 degrees.

2. Wash potatoes and dry them. Wrap them in foil and lay them in oven safe pan.

3. Cook potatoes until they are done. Test doneness by inserting a fork into potatoes.

4. Unwrap potatoes and cut a slit into each potato. Insert butter inside slits and let it melt inside the potatoes.

5. Add sour cream and bacon bits.

6. Mix barbecue sauce with pulled pork, stirring until blended well together.

7. Add 3 spoons of pulled pork on top of the potatoes. Eat warm.

Cheese Scalloped Potatoes

6 people

80"

Moderate

---

6 medium potatoes, sliced thinly
1 onion sliced thinly
2 cups of shredded sharp

cheddar cheese
1 tsp of garlic powder
Salt and pepper to taste
2 tsp of butter or margarine

1 ½ cups of milk

---

1. Preheat oven to 375 degrees. Spray the casserole dish with cooking spray.

2. Layer the potatoes at the bottom of the pan.

3. Follow with some onions and cheese. Repeat layers until the casserole dish is full.

4. Dot the top with butter and cut it into small pieces. Pour milk over the mixture.

5. Cover the casserole dish with foil and bake at 375 degrees for 1 hour or until bubbly and browned on top.

Fully Loaded Mashed Potatoes

8-10 people   45"   Easy

3 lbs. of potatoes, peeled and chopped	margarine	cubed
¾ cup of sour cream	1 tsp of Old Bay seasoning	½ lb. of cooked bacon, crumbled
1 pkg of cream cheese	1 tsp of soul food seasoning	2 tsp of parsley flakes
½ cup of milk	2 ½ cups of shredded sharp cheddar cheese	1 tsp of garlic salt
2 – 4 tbsps. of butter or	1 cup of Velveeta cheese,	1 mixer

1. Preheat oven to 350 degrees.

2. Place potatoes in a stock pot and cook until tender.

3. Drain potatoes and put them into a bowl.

4. Mix sour cream, cream cheese, milk, butter, ½ shredded cheese, Velveeta cheese, seasonings, and parsley flakes in the bowl.

5. Beat mixture on medium low speed until it is blended well.

6. Stir in bacon and onions.

7. Pour into greased baking dish and top with remaining cheese.

8. Bake for 30 minutes or until heated thoroughly and the cheese is melted. Enjoy.

Cheesy Squash Casserole

Psalm 91:10 (AMP) says, "No evil will befall you, Nor will any plague come near your tent."

6 - 8 people   40"   Easy

1 tbsp of vegetable oil
6 medium yellow squash/
zucchini squash thinly sliced
1 large Vidalia Onion
1 tbsp of butter or margarine

½ grated Parmesan Chee-
se or shredded Parmesan
cheese
1 cup of shredded cheddar
cheese

½ cup of sour cream
1 tsp of soul food seasoning
1 tsp of Old Bay seasoning
1 sleeve of Ritz crackers,
crushed

1. Preheat oven to 350 degrees. Grease a 2-quart heat safe dish.

2. Heat the oil in a large sauce pan over medium heat.

3. Sauté the squash, onions, and butter until soft.

4. Transfer to a bowl and stir in all cheeses and sour cream.

5. Add seasonings and stir until well mixed.

6. Place the mixture in a heat safe dish and sprinkle the crackers on top.

7. Bake for 30 minutes until the top is golden brown and bubbling.

8. 8. Let cool and serve.

Broccoli Casserole

3 pkg of frozen broccoli, chopped
¼ cup of sour cream
1 cup of sharp shredded cheddar cheese
1 cup of shredded parmesan cheese
¼ cup of Miracle Whip Salad dressing
1 can of condensed broccoli or mushroom soup
2 eggs, lightly beaten
2 cups Ritz crackers, crushed
2 tbsp of melted butter
1 tsp of Old Bay seasoning
1 tsp of soul food seasoning

8 people   45"   Easy

Psalm 91:9 (AMP) says, "Because you have made the LORD, (who is) my refuge, Even the Most High, your dwelling place."

1. Preheat oven to 350 degrees. Spray the glass baking dish with cooking spray.

2. Combine broccoli, salad dressing, cheese, soup, and eggs. Mix well. Place mixture in pan.

3. Top with crushed crackers and pour melted butter evenly over the crackers.

4. Bake for 35 minutes until browned.

Sausage and Potato Casserole

6 people   65"   Easy

3 cups of potatoes peeled, boiled, and cut into pieces
4 tbsp of butter
4 tbsp of flour
2 cups of milk
½ tsp of salt
¼ pepper

½ lb. Velveeta cheese diced
½ cup of sharp cheddar cheese, shredded
1 lb. of skinless smoked sausage
1/8 parsley flakes
1 tsp of Old Bay seasoning
1 tsp of soul food seasoning

1. Cut skinless smoked sausage in half, lengthwise, and then chop into ½ inch half-moons.

2. Cook in a frying pan for about 15 minutes, frequently turning to slightly brown.

3. Meanwhile, put cooked and diced potatoes in a 2-quart casserole. Add cooked meat and give it a gentle toss.

4. Mix all remaining ingredients, except for the shredded cheddar cheese and parsley, in a sauce pan over medium heat until warm, melted, and smooth (use a whisk and stir constantly).

5. Pour white cheese sauce over potatoes and meat. Sprinkle shredded sharp cheddar cheese on top, then sprinkle parsley over the top.

6. Bake in a preheated oven at 350 degrees for 35 to 45 minutes until golden brown on top.

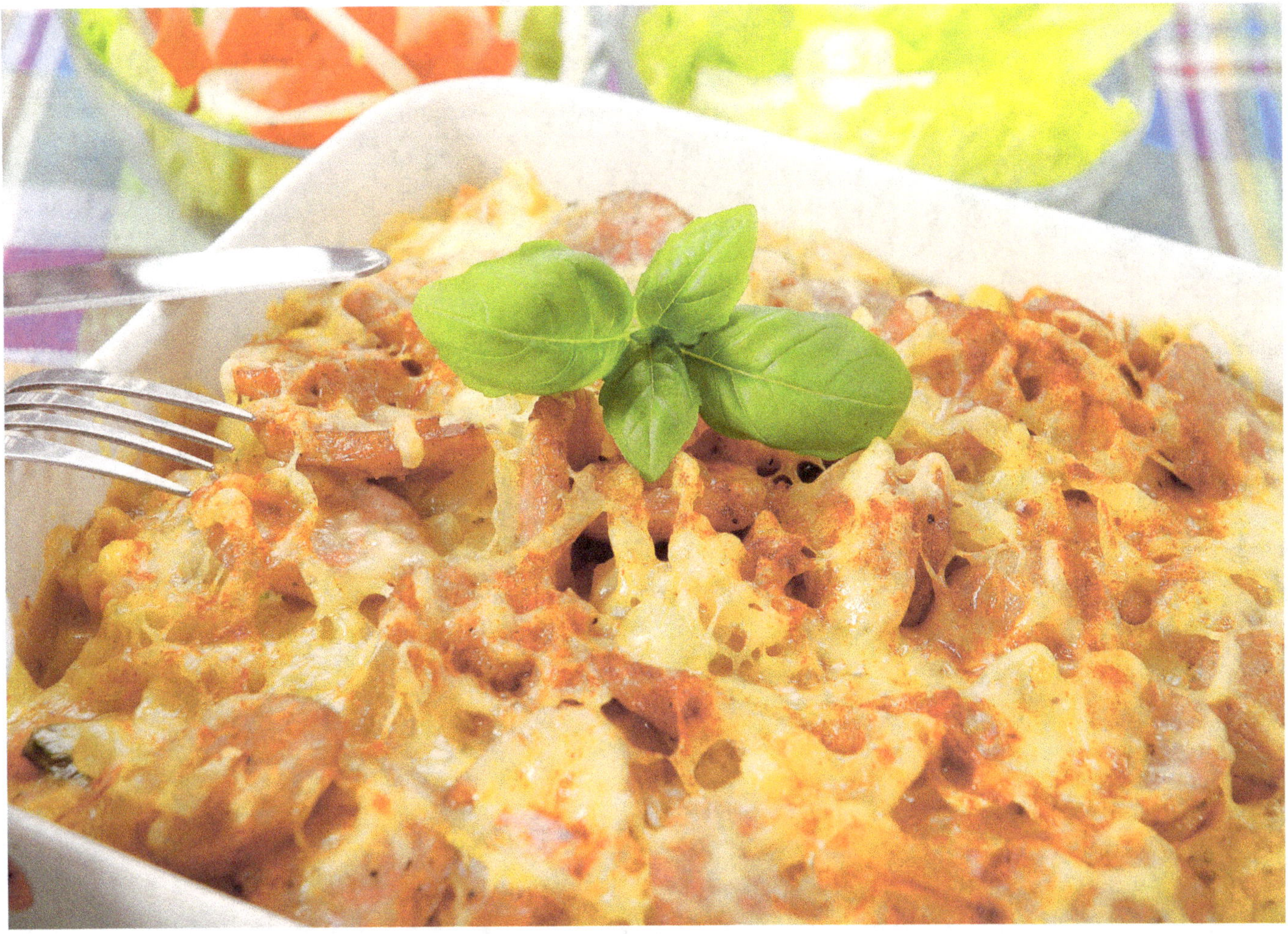

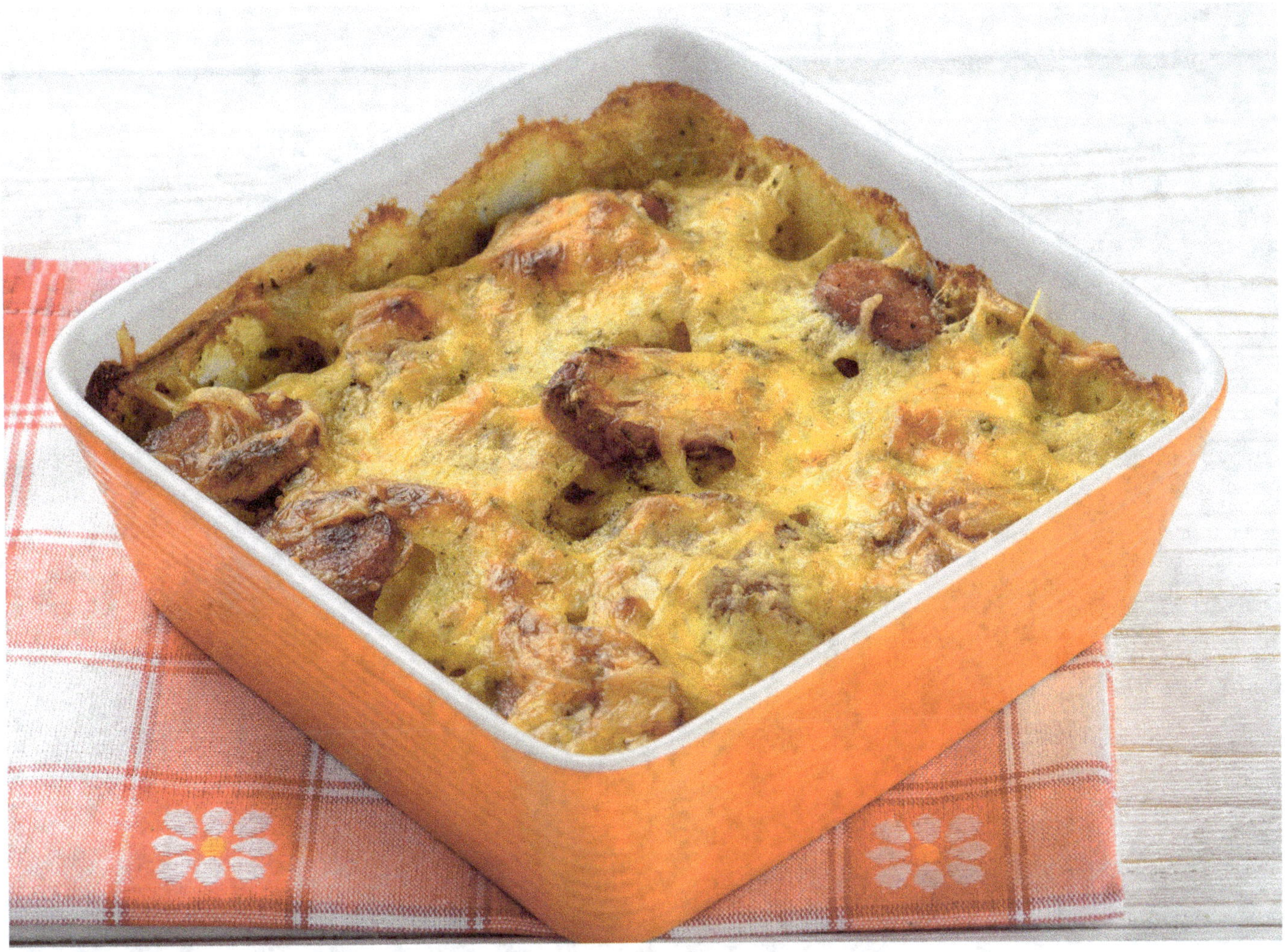

Chicken Pot Pie

6 people   50"   Easy

---

1 Rotisserie Chicken

1 can of mixed vegetables

1 can of cream of mushroom soup

1 can of cream of chicken

soup

1 deep dish pie crust

1 Pillsbury rolled pie crust

1 tbsp of Old Bay seasoning

1 tbsp of soul food seasoning

1 tbsp of melted butter

---

1. Preheat the oven to 350 degrees. Take the pie crusts out of the freezer and let them thaw out.

2. Pick the meat off the bones of the rotisserie chicken, cut it into pieces, and put it in a bowl.

3. Add mixed vegetables, all soups, and seasoning. Mix well and place inside of the deep dish pie crust.

4. Roll the pie crust out and lay it on top of the mixture. Try to seal the two pie crusts together and cut 2 slits on top of the crust.

5. Take the butter and brush it on top of the crust.

6. Bake for 35 minutes or until the top is browned.

Seafood Gumbo (scratch)

10 people   70"   Moderate

ROUX
2/3 cup of vegetable oil
½ cup of flour

---

2 small onions, chopped
3 cups of frozen okra
1 can of stewed tomatoes
2 tbsp of garlic salt
3 tbsp of butter or margarine

2 stalks of celery
6 cups of water
Accent salt and black pepper to taste
2 tsp of Cajun seasoning
1 tsp of Old Bay seasoning
6 chicken bouillon cubes
½ cup of parsley flakes or fresh
2 lbs. of shrimp deveined

and cleaned
5 potatoes, peeled and diced
1 cup of sausage cut into pieces
1 lb. of crab claws or legs
4 cups of cooked white rice
3 tbsp of corn starch. Add 1 ½ tbsp of water to make a paste.

---

1. In a small stock pot, put oil and flour together on low to medium heat until the flour starts to brown the color you want it. Set aside off the heat.

2. In a small frying pan or stock pot on medium heat, add butter, shrimp, garlic, and seasonings. Cook until the shrimp is pink. Remove from heat.

3. In a large stock pot, add water, potatoes, celery, sausages, onion, and crab legs. Cook until the potatoes are tender.

4. Add okra, tomatoes, parsley, bouillon cubes, and shrimp to the mixture. Stir until everything is mixed together well.

5. Let it simmer between low to medium heat for 30 minutes. Stirring occasionally to prevent sticking.

6. Add roux to the mixture and stir it to mix it well. If it is not as thick as you would like, add 3 tbsp of cornstarch paste to thicken it.

7. Let it simmer for 10 more minutes on low heat.

8. Let it cool and serve on top of cooked rice. Enjoy!

Seafood Gumbo (with Gumbo Mix)

Acts 4:12 (AMP) says, "And there is salvation in no one else; for there is no other name under heaven that has been given among people by which we must be saved (for God has provided the world no alternative for salvation)."

7 people   60"   Easy

---

4 tbsp of butter or margarine
1 lb. of smoked sausages finely chopped
1 lb. of cooked shrimp, deveined, cut up

3 ¾ cups of water
6 chicken bouillon cubes
1 box of gumbo mix and seasoning
1 small onion, chopped fine

1 tsp of Cajun seasoning
1 tsp of Old Bay seasoning
1 lb. of crab meat in a can, drained, or flake crab

---

1. First, melt the butter in a skillet on medium heat.

2. Drop in smoked sausages, shrimp, and onions. Cook until lightly browned.

3. Add water in the pot, bouillon cubes, and seasonings. Stir everything together and mix well.

4. Bring to a boil and add the box of Gumbo mix. Stir and cover the pot and let it cook until the rice is tender but still has water in the pot.

5. Add the crab and stir to make sure it is not sticking. Recover the pot and cook for 5 more minutes or until the water evaporates.

6. Let rice stand for 5 minutes after it finishes cooking.

7. Fluff the rice with a fork. Enjoy!

Shrimp Fried Rice

Psalm 35:2 (AMP) says, "Take hold of shield and buckler (small shield) And stand up for my help."

6 people	35"	Easy

4 oz frozen uncooked deveined shrimp
1 tsp of Old Bay seasoning
1 tsp of soul food seasoning
1 tsp of garlic
1 tsp of Cajun seasoning

3 tbsp of butter or margarine
1 medium Vidalia Onion, cut up in small pieces
4 eggs scrambled
½ garden peas
4 cups of cooked rice

4 to 5 tbsp of vegetable oil for stir frying
2 tbsp of soy sauce
1 tbsp of Worcestershire sauce

1. In a frying pan on medium heat, add butter, shrimp, all seasonings, garlic salt, and onion. Cook until onions are translucent.

2. Add garden peas, cooked rice, soy sauce, and Worcestershire sauce.

3. Scramble eggs in a separate skillet. Put eggs with the other mixture and stir it up well.

4. Let it warm all the way through. Serve.

The sweetness of the Vidalia onion really brings the flavor of the shrimp fried rice to life. Amazing flavor.

Fried Salmon Patties

1 can of salmon, any brand
1 small onion cut into small pieces
Salt and pepper to taste
3 tbsp of flour
4 tbsp of meal
1 egg
2 cups of vegetable oil
1 tsp of Old Bay seasoning
½ tsp of soul food seasoning

6 people | 45" | Easy

Psalm 34:8 (AMP) says, "O taste and see that the LORD (our God) is good; How blessed (fortunate, prosperous, and favored by God) is the man who takes refuge in Him."

1. Put a medium size skillet with 2 cups oil on low heat.

2. Pick the bones out of the salmon after opening the can.

3. Break up the salmon with a fork and add onion, flour, meal, egg, and seasonings.

4. Make the salmon up into patties.

5. Turn the heat up on the skillet to medium. When it starts to heat up, place the patties in heated oil.

6. When the patties are golden brown on one side, turn them over to the other side and let them brown.

7. Drain them on paper towels.

This recipe is so good and flavorful.

Seafood Dressing

10 - 20 people   80"   Moderate

Romans 6:1 (AMP) says, "WHAT SHALL we say (to all this)? Should we continue in sin and practice sin as a habit so that (God's gift of) grace may increase and overflow?"

2 8 oz cornbread dressing mix
3 tbsp of butter or margarine
1 can of cream of chicken/mushroom soup
½ cup of diced celery
2 8 oz cans of oyster, smoked
2 pkg of flake crab meat or can crab meat

½ tsp of black pepper
1 tbsp of poultry seasoning
1 tbsp of Old Bay seasoning
1 tbsp of soul food seasoning
1 ½ tsp of dried parsley
1 deep dish tin pan
1 14.5 oz of chicken broth or broth from turkey wings or hen

1. Preheat oven to 350 degrees.

2. Put corn bread mix in a tin pan.

3. Pour half of the broth on top of the corn bread mix so it can soak up the flavor of the broth.

4. Add another stock pot on high heat and place eggs in water to boil.

5. Add butter in another skillet on medium heat. Add onions, parsley, shrimp, oysters, celery, and seasonings.

6. Cook shrimp until it is pink and all the butter has been absorbed into the food.

7. Remove from heat and cut the shrimp and oysters into little pieces.

8. Mix the corn bread dressing with the seafood mixture. Stir until well mixed together.

9. Peel and cut up eggs to go into the mixture. Stir and add more broth until you get the mixture good and moist.

10. Add 1 can of cream of chicken/mushroom soup and stir to blend together. The dressing should be at desired consistency.

11. Cover the tin pan with foil, place in the oven, and cook for 55 minutes or until the top is golden brown and bubbling.

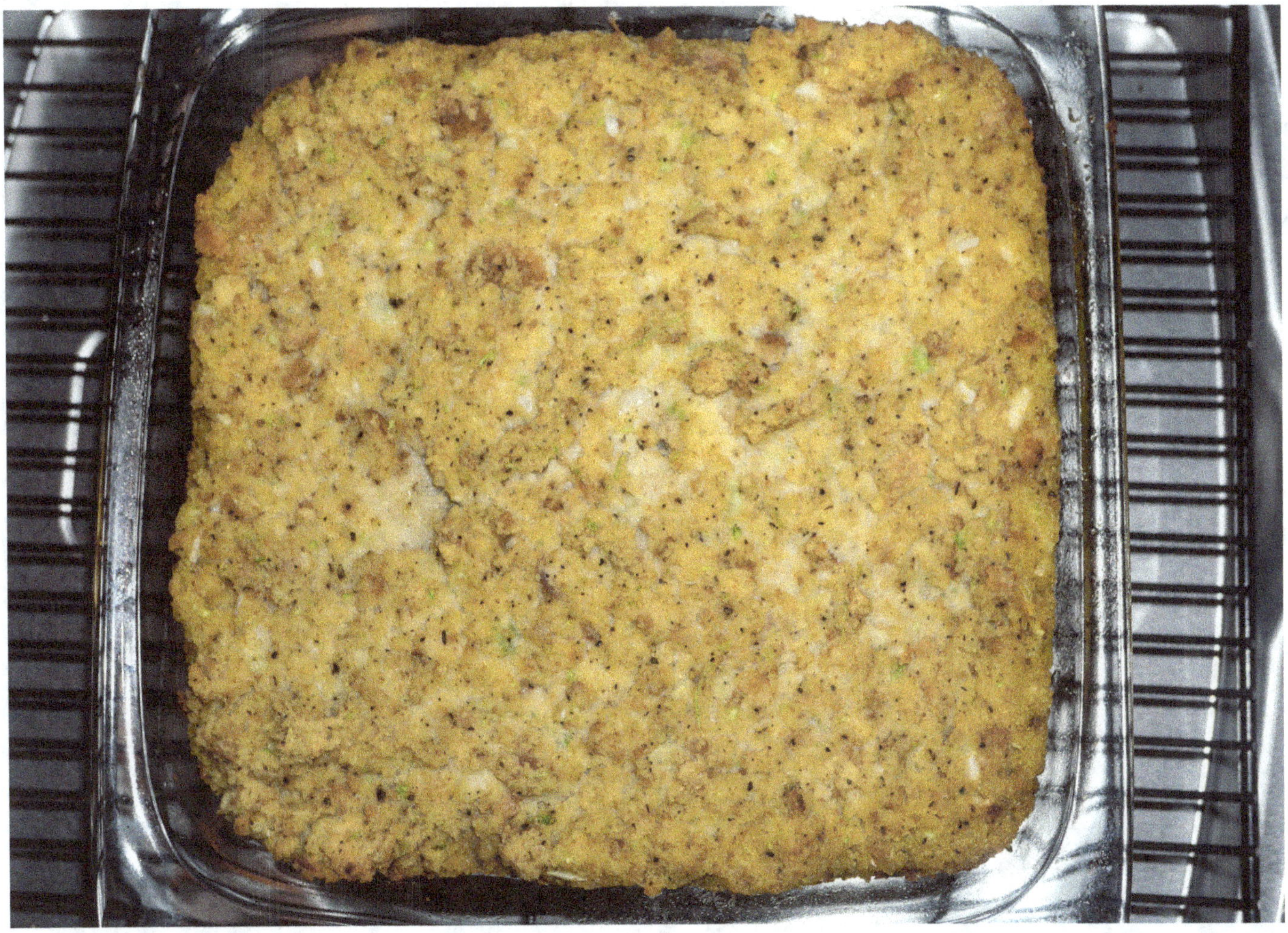

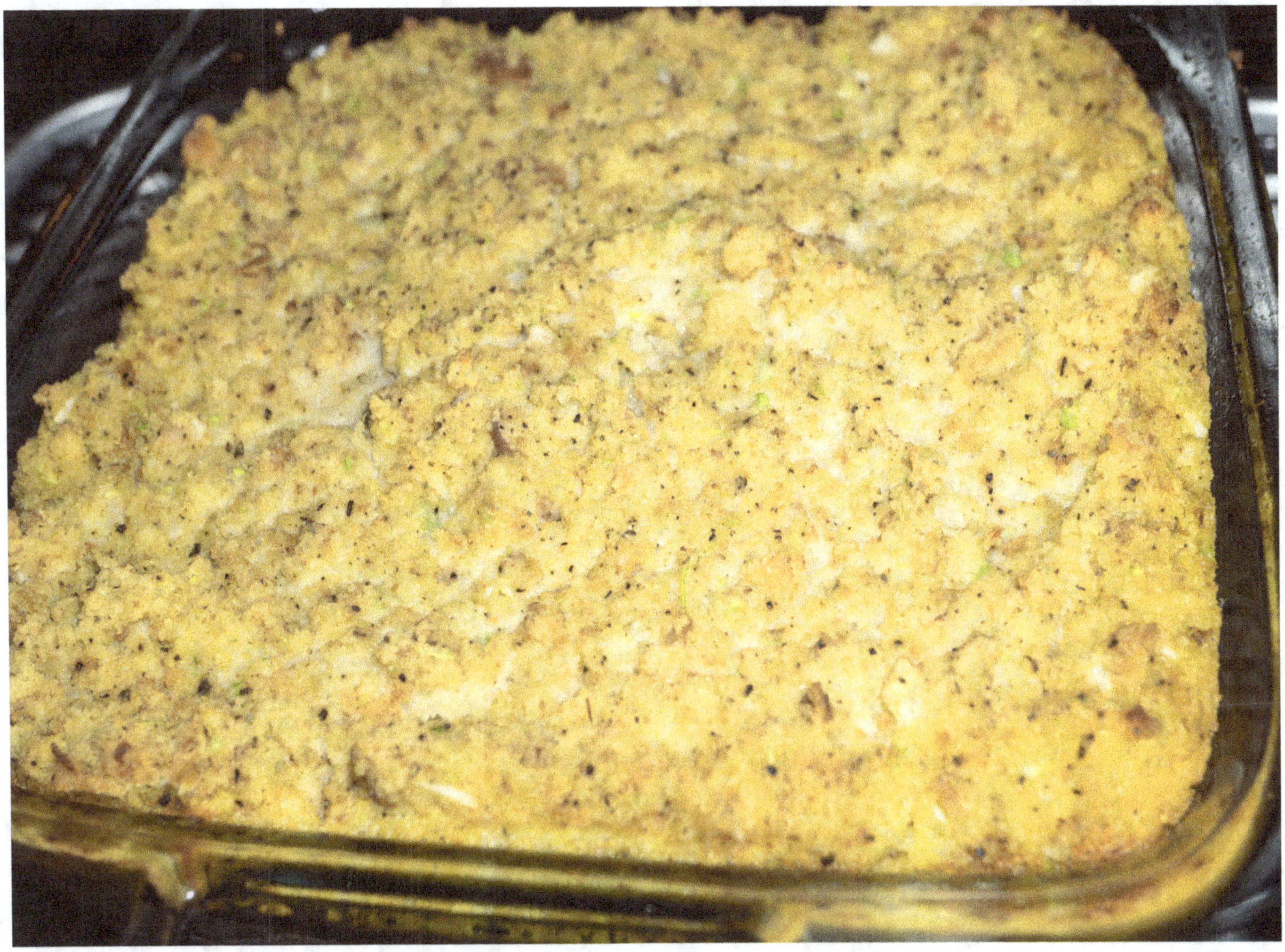

Shrimp and Grits

Romans 8:10 (AMP) says, "If Christ lives in you, though your (natural) body is dead because of sin, your spirit is alive because of righteousness (which He provides)."

This is so delicious.

6 - 8 people   50"   Moderate

---

1 lb. of shrimp deveined, peeled
1/3 cup of flour
¼ cup of butter
¼ cup of vegetable oil

1 tbsp of parsley flakes
1 tsp of Old Bay seasoning
1 tsp of soul food seasoning
1 tsp of Cajun seasoning
1 tsp of garlic powder

6 chicken bouillon cubes
4 pkg of instant grits
16 oz of water for gravy
3 cups of water for grits
1/3 cup of milk

---

1. In a skillet on medium heat, add butter, shrimp, garlic, and other seasonings.

2. Cook until the shrimp is pink. Remove them from the pan.

3. Add ¼ cup of vegetable oil to the pan on medium heat. Let the pan get hot, add flour to the oil, and brown the flour for the gravy.

4. After the gravy is medium brown, add 10 oz of water to the mixture and 6 crushed chicken bouillon cubes. Cook it down with the lid on, stirring it occasionally, so it doesn't stick to the pan.

5. Turn down the heat to low and let simmer.

6. Get a glass dish that is microwave safe. Pour grits into the dish, add 2 cups of wa-ter, and stir until well mixed.

7. Put glass dish inside of the microwave for 10 minutes, occasionally stirring to prevent sticking.

8. Taste grits to see if they are creamy enough for you. If they are not done enough, just add 1/3 cup more water and cook 10 more minutes.

9. Add 1/3 cup of milk and put back into the microwave for 4 more minutes.

10. Let stand and cool. Gravy should be done at this time. Turn off the heat.

11. Serve grits with shrimp gravy on top of it.

Baked Tilapia

6 people   35"   Easy

1 cup of seasoned bread-crumbs	1 tbsp of parsley flakes	1 tbsp of Cajun seasoning
6 pieces of tilapia fish	2 tbsp of Old Bay seasoning	1 pack of ranch dressing mix
	2 tbsp of soul food seasoning	Olive oil spray

1. Preheat oven to 350 degrees.

2. In a bowl, combine breadcrumbs, parsley, and seasonings. Cover the fish on both sides, then sprinkle the ranch dressing mix on top of the seasonings.

3. Spray the glass pan with olive oil cooking spray.

4. Put the seasoned fish into the pan and put it into the oven.

5. Bake uncovered for 10 to 15 minutes or until fish flakes easily with a fork.

Salmon Honey Bake

6-8 people   40"   Easy

¼ cup of honey
1 tbsp of garlic salt
4 tsp of honey mustard
1 large salmon filet

1 tbsp of soul food seasoning
1 tbsp of Old Bay seasoning

1 tbsp of Cajun seasoning
2 tbsp of olive oil

1. Preheat oven to 375 degrees.

2. Line a baking sheet with foil.

3. In a small bowl, mix honey, garlic salt, olive oil, honey mustard, and all seasonings.

4. Place the salmon in a baking dish lined with foil and spread the mix onto the length of the salmon.

5. Close the edges of the foil together, sealing the ends.

6. Cook for 15 to 20 minutes until done.

7. Remove from oven and let cool. Then serve.

Fried Tilapia

Psalm 33:4 (AMP) says, "For the word of the LORD is right; And all His work is done in faithfulness."

6 - 8 people　　35"　　Easy

---

6 or 7 pieces of tilapia fish	1 tbsp of soul food seasoning	2 cups of fish meal
1 tbsp of Old Bay seasoning	1 tbsp of Cajun Seasoning	2 cups of vegetable oil

---

1. In a skillet on medium heat, put in 2 cups of vegetable oil and let it heat until it is hot.

2. While you are waiting on the grease to get hot enough, wash the 6 pieces of fish and season it on both sides with the seasonings. The grease should be hot.

3. Place the fish meal in a gallon zip lock bag. Drop the seasoned pieces of fish down in the meal and shake to coat the pieces of fish.

4. Take the fish, put it into oil, and fry them until they are golden brown on each side. Take out and let drain on a pan with paper towels inside it.

5. After the fish is done, cut the heat off and serve the fish hot.

Low Country Boil

1 lb. of shrimp deveined
2 lb. of snow crab legs
1 lb. of pork sausages
10 large, boiled eggs and shells removed
6 large potatoes peeled, cubed
1 pkg of Old Bay seasoning packet
2 tbsp of soul food seasoning
2 tbsp of Cajun seasoning
½ cup of Tony Chachere's injectables marinade
roasted garlic and herb
10 bouillon chicken cubes
5 corns on the cob
6 cups of water

10 - 15 people   75"   Moderate

Matthew 6:33 (AMP) says, "But most first and most importantly seek (aim at, strive after) His kingdom and His righteousness (His way of doing and being right—the attitude and character of God), and all these things will be given to you also."

1. In an extra-large stock pot, put 6 cups of water on medium heat.

2. Add potatoes, corn on the cob, sausages, a package of Old Bay seasoning, other seasonings, and chicken bouillon cubes. Cook until the potatoes are almost done.

3. Add shrimp, crab legs, eggs, and injectable marinade to the pot.

4. Continue to cook until the shrimp and crab are done.

5. Turn off the heat, let it sit, and soak up the flavors for 30 minutes.

6. It should be cool enough to eat in 25 minutes. Enjoy.

Leftovers can be kept in the refrigerator for a couple of days.

This can be refrigerated or frozen.

Italian Flavored Meatloaf

8 people   70"   Easy

Romans 8:24 (AMP) says, "For in this hope we were saved (by faith). But hope (the object of) which is seen is not hope. For who hopes for what he already sees?"

1 lb. of hamburger meat
1 pkg of Zesty Italian dressing mix
2 tbsp of Worcestershire sauce
1 tbsp of Old Bay seasoning
1 tbsp of soul food seasoning
2 eggs beaten
2 tbsp of ketchup
½ cup of ketchup (topping)

1. Preheat oven to 350 degrees.

2. In a bowl, combine hamburger meat, zesty Italian dressing mix, Worcestershire sauce, other seasonings, eggs, and ketchup. Mix up with your hands until everything is well mixed in hamburger meat.

3. Take a glass loaf pan and put hamburger mix inside the loaf pan. Press down the hamburger meat to take the form of the loaf pan.

4. Place it in a hot oven to cook for 45 minutes to 1 hour until done all the way through.

5. After it is done, spread the extra ketchup on top of it evenly and put it back into the oven for 10 more minutes until the ketchup sets.

6. Enjoy.

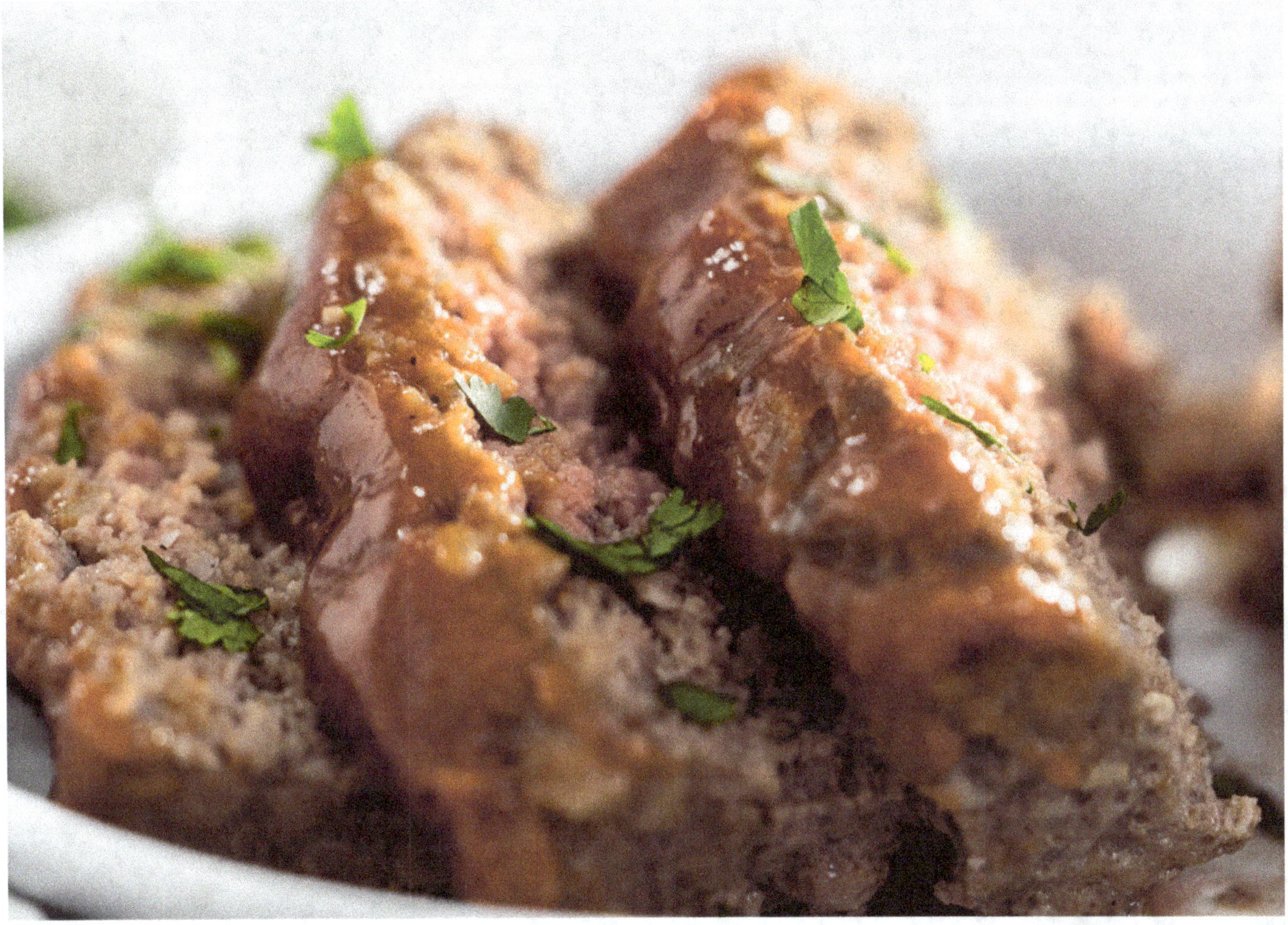
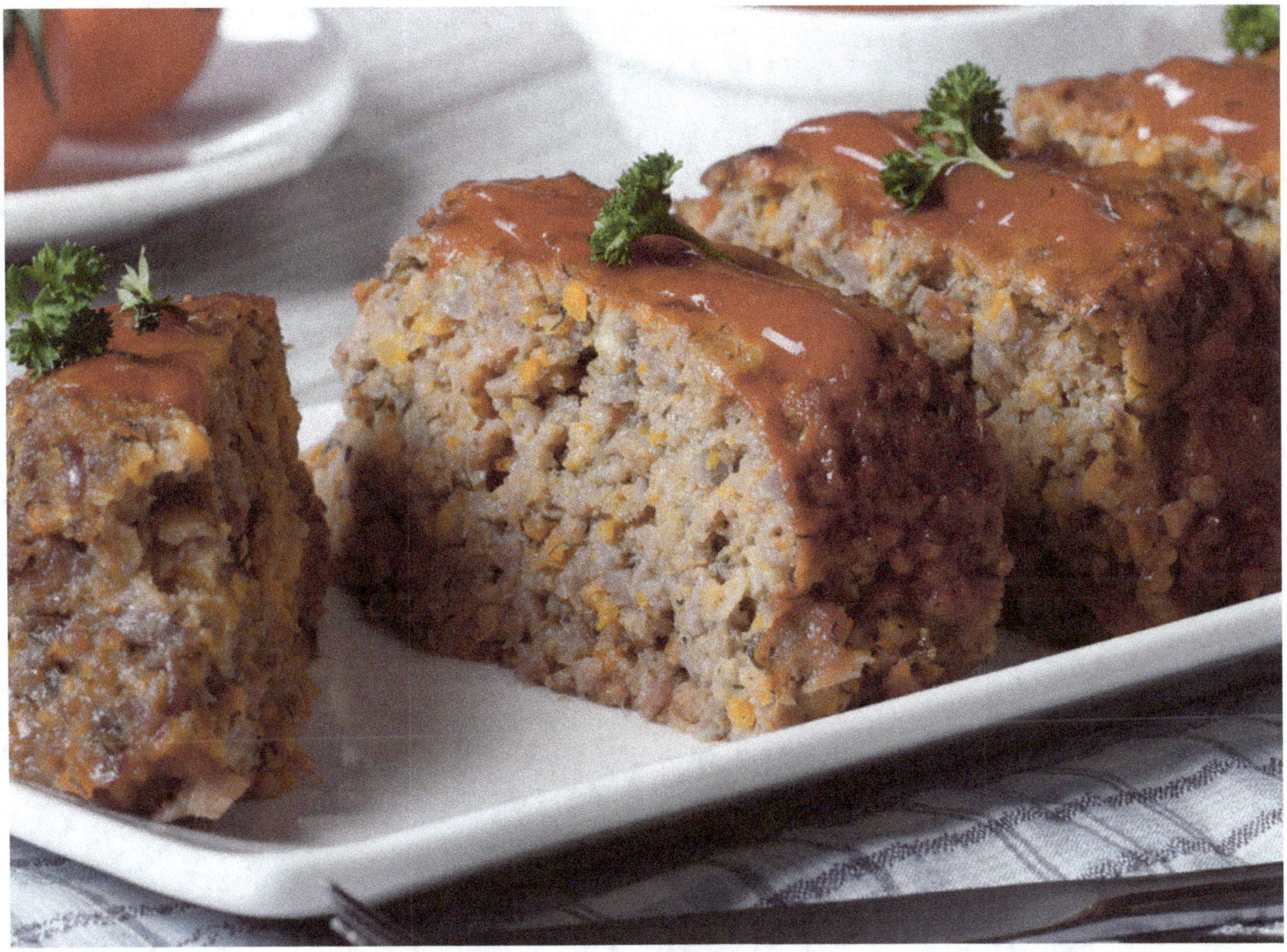

Loaded Meatloaf

7 people   70"   Easy

Leftovers can be refrigerated or frozen.

1 lb. of hamburger meat
1 pkg of Goya seasoning ham flavor
3 tbsp of Worcestershire
sauce
2 eggs, slightly scrambled
1 tsp of Old Bay seasoning
1 tsp of soul food seasoning
1 lb. of bacon cooked and crumbled up
2 tsp of Ketchup
1 bottle of Ketchup

1. Preheat the oven to 350 degrees.

2. In a large bowl, combine the hamburger meat and all the remaining ingredients.

3. Mix them together well and place in a loaf pan or glass dish. Form it in a mound or loaf shape.

4. Place it in the hot oven and cook for 50 minutes or until done all the way through.

5. After it is done, take it out of the oven, squeeze the rest of the ketchup on the top of it, and smooth it out.

6. Place it back into the oven for 10 more minutes for the Ketchup to set. Enjoy!

Hamburger Steak with Gravy

Proverbs 15:8b (AMP) says, "But the prayer of the upright is His delight."

8 people   90"   Easy

---

1 lb. of hamburger meat
3 tbsp of Worcestershire sauce
1 tsp of Old Bay seasoning

1 tsp of soul food seasoning
1 pkg of Goya seasoning ham flavor
2 eggs

4 tbsp of flour
1/3 cup of vegetable oil
2 ½ cups of water
Salt and pepper to taste

---

1. Place hamburger meat in a large bowl.

2. Add all the ingredients except flour and mix it together until everything is mixed well in the hamburger meat. You may have to use your hands to get it mixed up good.

3. Make hamburger patties out of the hamburger meat. You will usually get 6 or more patties out of the hamburger meat.

4. Put 1/3 cup of vegetable oil in a pan on medium heat. Place hamburger patties in oil once it is hot.

5. Cook the hamburger patties until they are brown on both sides and on the inside. Remove the patties out of the oil and put them on paper towels to drain the excess fat.

6. Put the flour into the hot grease and stir flour until it starts to brown the color that you desire.

7. Add water to the mixture and stir to make sure the gravy will be smooth and well mixed.

8. Place the patties back into the gravy, turn the heat down, and let them simmer for 30 to 45 minutes. Stir occasionally to prevent sticking.

9. After the gravy has thickened, cut the heat off, and serve with rice or mashed potatoes.

Baked Oxtails

Proverbs 19:21 (AMP) says, "Many plans are in a man's mind, But it is the LORD's purpose for him that will stand (be carried out)."

8 people   70"   Moderate

They are so good.

1 lb. of oxtails, washed
1 cup of flour
2 tbsp of Old Bay seasoning
2 tbsp of soul food sea-

soning
2 cups of vegetable oil
2 cups of water
5 beef bouillon cubes, crushed

1 cup of flour
4 tbsp of flour
Salt and pepper to taste

1. Preheat the oven to 350 degrees.

2. In a large skillet, add vegetable oil and put it on medium heat.

3. Mix oxtails and seasonings. Season each oxtail on the front and back.

4. Put 1 cup of flour in a gallon freezer bag. Put oxtails in flour and coat really good.

5. Place the oxtails in hot grease and brown on both sides of them. Take them out of the grease and place them in a tin pan.

6. After every one of the oxtails are browned on each side, place them on paper towels to soak up excess oil.

7. Pour out most of the grease except 1/3 cup. Place the rest of the flour in the skillet and stir the flour as it begins to turn brown. When it turns the desired color, add water and beef bouillon cubes to the flour solution. Let it begin to boil just slightly. Begin to stir to a smooth consistency.

8. Place the oxtails in a baking tin pan and pour the gravy over the oxtails. Cook them on 350 degrees for 45 minutes until the meat falls off the bones.

9. Enjoy. They can be served with rice or mashed potatoes.

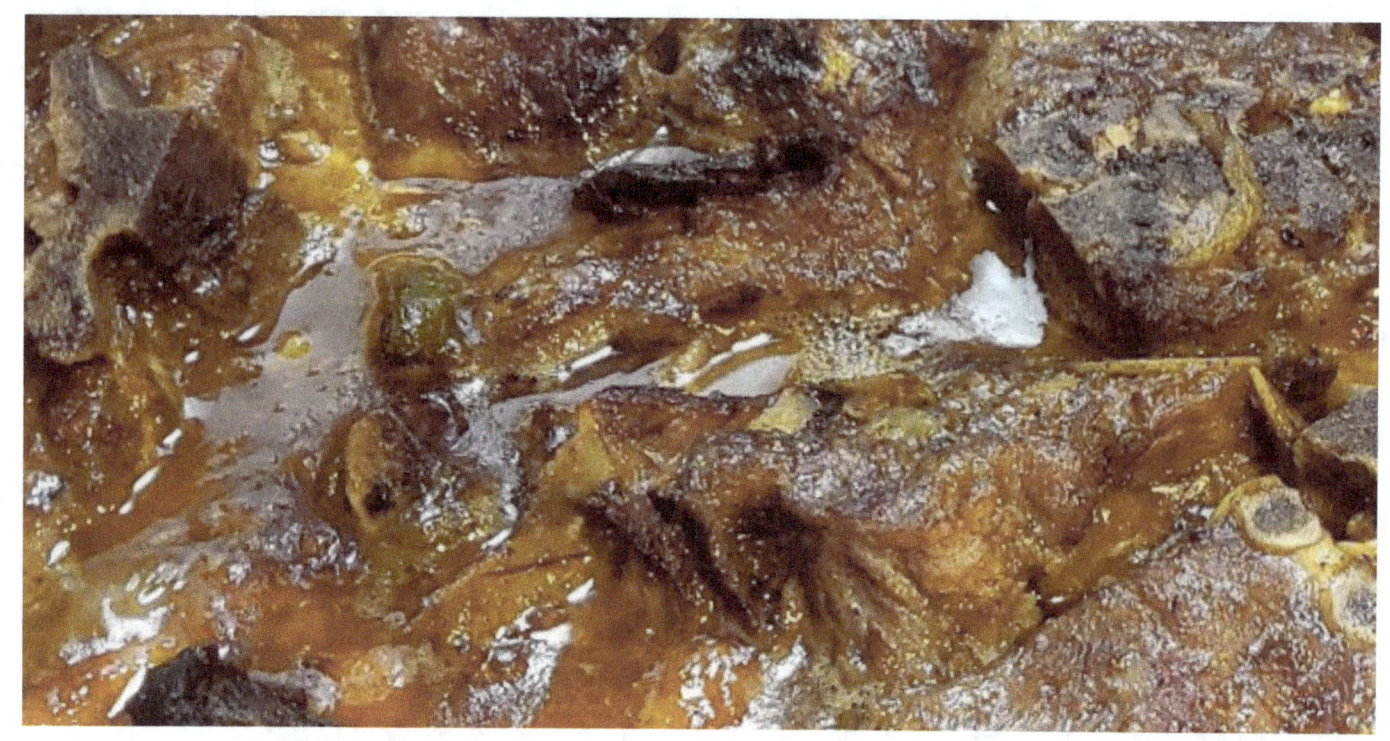

Baked Beef Neckbones

Romans 12:19 (AMP) says, "Beloved never avenge yourselves but leave the way open for God's wrath (and His judicial righteousness); for it is written (in Scripture), "VENGEANCE IS MINE, I WILL REPAY," says the Lord."

8 people   60"   Moderate

2 lb. of beef neck bones, washed	2 cups of water	2 tbsp of cornstarch (mixed with water to form a paste)
2 tbsp of soul food seasoning	2 packs of brown gravy mix	
2 tbsp of Old Bay seasoning	5 beef bouillon cubes, crushed	

1. Preheat the oven to 350 degrees.

2. In a tin pan, spread out the beef neckbones along the bottom of the pan.

3. Start seasoning the meat with Old Bay seasoning and soul food seasoning mixture. Season both sides of the meat with seasonings.

4. Take 2 packs of gravy mix and place them in a small bowl. Mix them with a cup of water each. Whisk the gravy around so it can be mixed up really well with no lumps in it.

5. Pour both of the gravy mixes over the beef neck bones in a pan. Add the beef bouillon cubes to the mixture.

6. Make sure the water is covering the neck bones. If not, add more water until the water covers them.

7. Place foil on top of the pan and place in a hot oven to cook for 50 minutes or until the meat is tender and falling off the bones.

8. After they are done, see if the gravy is thickened. If not, add the cornstarch paste and stir as you are pouring it.

9. Place back in the oven for 10 more minutes. Take out once the gravy has thickened.

10. Serve. It is great with rice or mashed potatoes.

Seared Steaks

4 T-bone steaks, washed
Montreal Steak Seasonings
4 beef bouillon cubes, crushed
3 tbsp of Worcestershire sauce
Grill
Cooking timer
foil

4 people   35"   Easy

Romans 15:13 (AMP) says, "May the God of hope fill you with all joy and peace in believing (through the experience of your faith) that by the power of the Holy Spirit you will abound in hope and overflow with confidence in His Promises."

1. Heat grill as directed.

2. Take T bone steaks and take a knife. Make small cuts in the front and back of the steaks.

3. Season steaks with steak seasoning and beef bouillon seasoning on the front and back of the steaks. Add Worcestershire sauce to both sides of the steak.

4. The grill is hot and distribute the coals so they will cook evenly.

5. Lay steaks on a cleaned grill. Close the top of the grill and set the timer for 8 to 10 minutes. Cook steaks for 10 minutes or until brown on the side.

6. Turn steaks on the other side and cook for 10 more minutes or until brown.

7. Cut steaks to see if it is cooked on the inside. If it is not, cook to your taste. Wrap each steak individually up in foil and let sit on the grill until all of the steak is ready.

8. Continue to cook in foil. Also, juices will collect in foil and the steak will be tender. Take steaks off the grill. Enjoy.

Baked Beef Stew

8 people   70"   Moderate

1 lb. of brisket and all beef, beef stew mixed, washed
3 tbsp of Old Bay seasoning
3 tbsp of soul food seasoning
3 cups of water
6 beef bouillon cubes, crushed
2 packages of brown gravy mix, any variety
3 tbsp of cornstarch (mix with 1 tbsp water to make a paste)

1. Preheat oven to 350 degrees.

2. In a tin pan, place the beef stew along the bottom of the pan.

3. Season them with Old Bay seasoning and soul food seasoning mixture.

4. In a bowl, combine the 2 packs of brown gravy mix with 2 cups of water and whisk to blend it together. Pour gravy mix over into the pan. Make sure the water is covering the beef stew. If not, add more water until the water covers the beef stew.

5. Cook the beef stew for 45 minutes until done and the meat falls off the bones.

6. Check the consistency of the gravy. If it is too runny, stir in the cornstarch paste to thicken the gravy.

7. Place the beef stew back into the oven for 10 more minutes to help thicken the gravy.

8. After the gravy is thickened, take it out of the oven. Enjoy. Serve with rice or mashed potatoes.

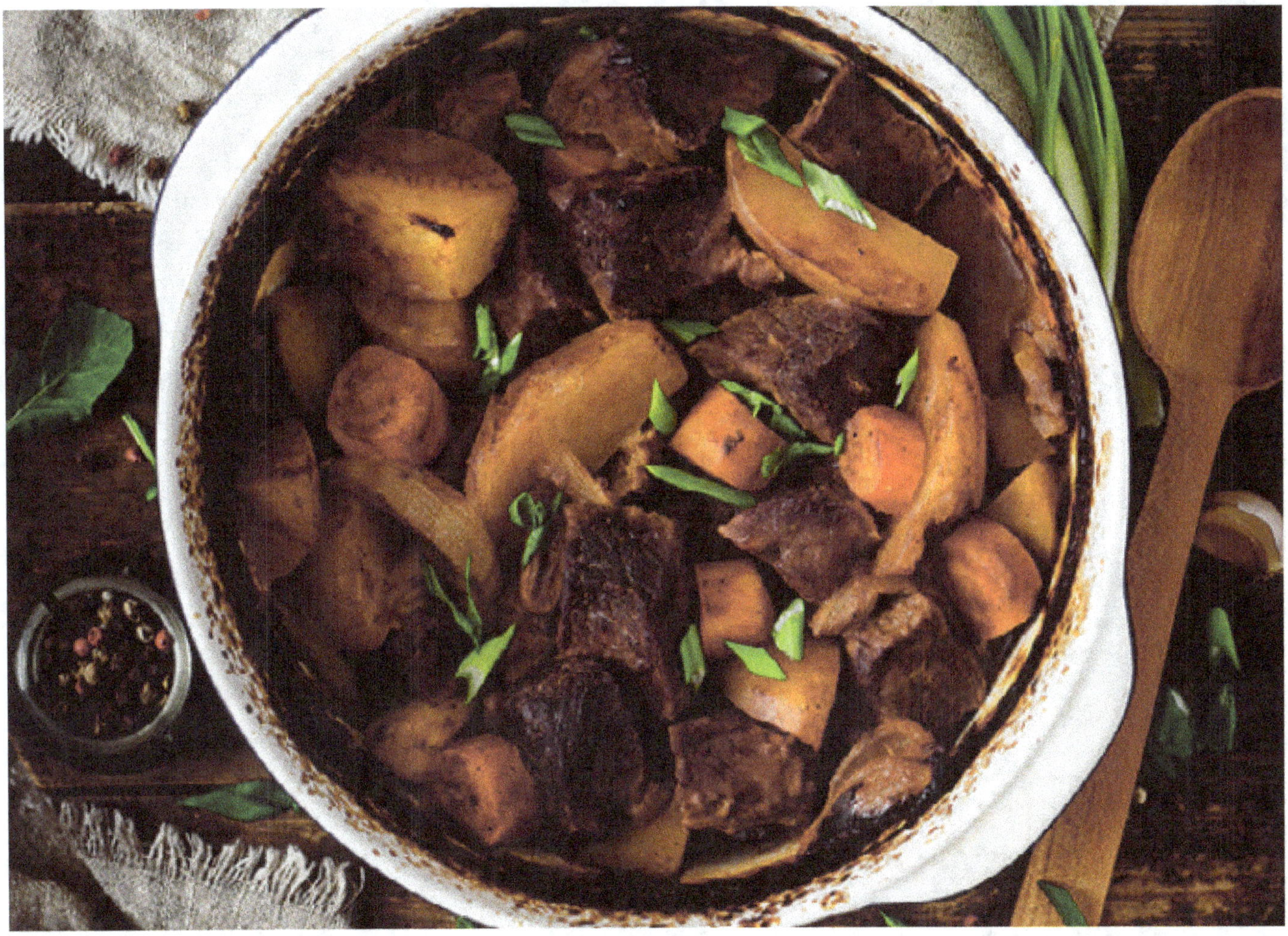

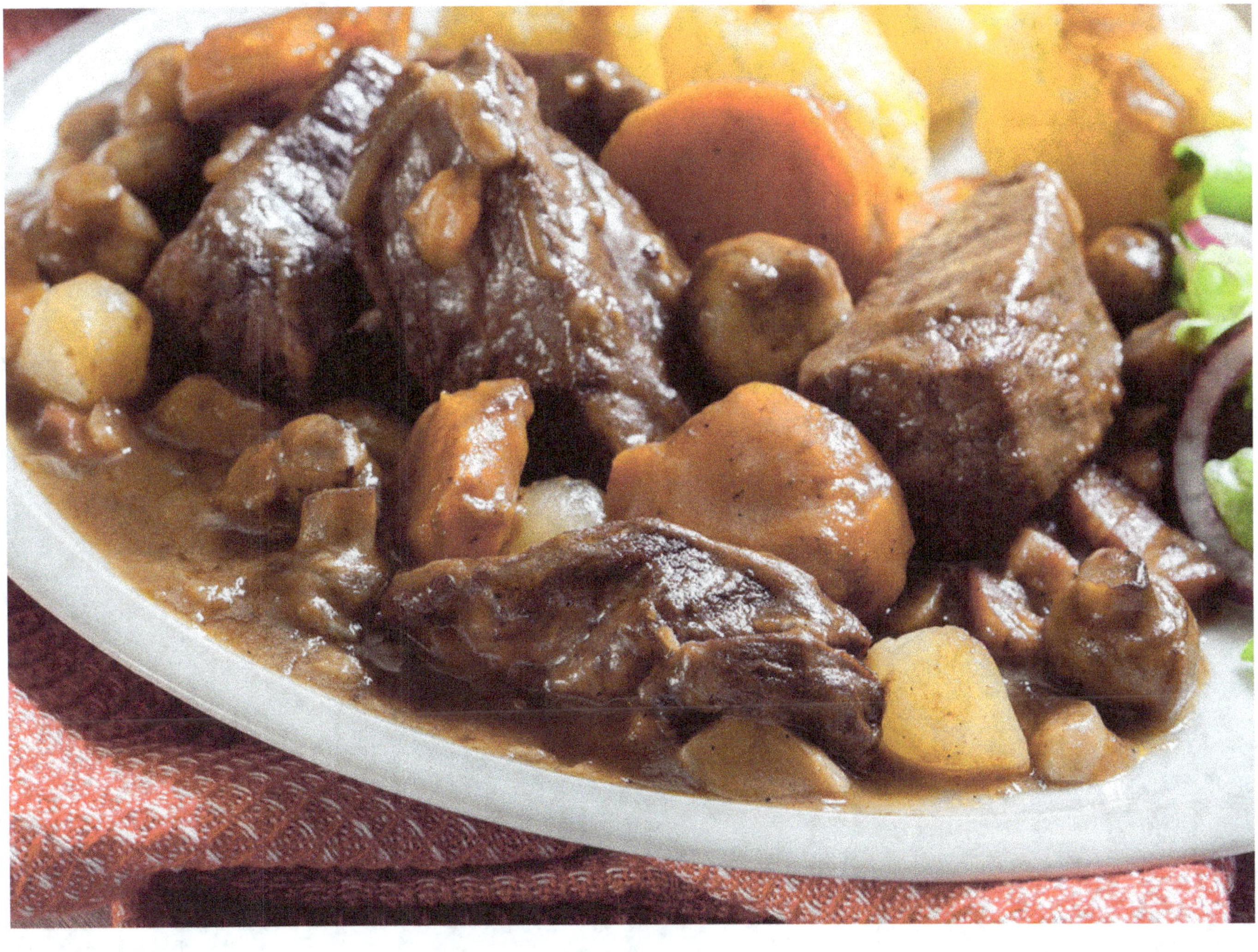

Lemon Pepper Chicken Wings

1 Corinthians 2:9 (AMP) says, "but just as it is written (in Scripture). "THINGS WHICH THE EYE HAS NOT SEEN AND THE EAR HAVE NOT HEARD, AND WHICH HAVE NOT ENTERED THE HEART OF MAN. ALL THAT GOD HAS PREPARED FOR THOSE WHO LOVE HIM (who hold Him in affectionate reverence, who obey Him, and who gratefully recognize the benefits that He has bestowed)."

8 people   60"   Easy

---

1 lb. of Chicken wingettes,   mix   Foil
separated, washed   1 tsp of Old Bay seasoning
Lemon pepper seasoning   1 tsp of soul food seasoning

---

1. Preheat the oven to 350 degrees.

2. Place wingettes in an oven safe pan. Line the pan with foil.

3. Season wingettes with Old Bay and soul seasoning on the front and back.

4. Apply the lemon pepper seasoning last on the front and back.

5. Cover the pan with foil and bake for 30 minutes.

6. Remove the foil and bake for 10 more minutes.

Montreal Steak Chicken Wings

1 Corinthians 3:9 (AMP) says, "For we are God's fellow workers (His servants working together); you are God's cultivated field (His garden, His vineyard), God's building."

8 people

60"

Easy

---

1 lb. of chicken wingettes, washed
1 tbsp of soul food seaso-

ning
1 tbsp of Old Bay seaso-
ning

Montreal Steak seasoning
Foil

---

1. Preheat oven to 350 degrees.

2. Place wingettes in an oven safe pan lined with foil. Place wingettes along bottom of the pan.

3. Season wingettes with Old Bay and soul food seasoning on the front and back of them. Then add Montreal steak seasoning to wings on the front

and back of them.

4. Cover the pan with foil and place in a hot oven. Cook wings for 30 minutes with foil. Then remove foil and cook for 10 more minutes uncovered.

Sazon Goya Chicken Wingettes

1 Corinthians 4:20 (AMP) says, "For the kingdom of God is not based on talk but on power."

8 people   60"   Easy

1 lb. of chicken winget-
tes, washed
1 tbsp of soul food sea-
soning
1 tbsp Old Bay seaso-
ning

4 packs of Sazon Goya,
(Hispanic) seasoning
Foil

1. Preheat oven to 350 degrees.

2. Place wingettes in an oven safe pan. Place wingettes along the bottom of the pan.

3. Season the front and back of the wingettes with the Old Bay seasoning and soul food seasoning.

4. Next, open the packs of Sazon Goya Seasoning and season the front and back of the wingettes. The wings will have an orange appearance on them. This is normal.

5. Cover the top of the pan with foil and bake for 30 minutes covered. Then uncover the wingettes and bake for 10 more minutes uncovered. Enjoy.

Barbecue Chicken Wings

1 Corinthians 3:16 (AMP) says, "Do you not know and understand that you (the church) are the temple of God, and that the Spirit of God dwells (permanently) in you (collectively and individually)?"

8 people	50"	Easy

1 ½ lb. of chicken thighs, washed

4 tbsp of soul food seasoning

4 tbsp of Old Bay seasoning

1 cup of water

1 bottle of barbecue sauce,

any flavor

Foil

1. Preheat the oven to 350 degrees.

2. Place the chicken in an oven safe pan. Season the front and the back of the chicken with soul food and Old Bay seasoning.

3. Pour 1/2 cup of water into the baking dish to keep the chicken from sticking to the pan.

4. Place the chicken in the oven and cover it with foil and cook for 45 minutes or until the chicken is done.

5. 5. Cut into the chicken to make sure it is not still pink. Pour off any excess juices, only leaving a small amount in the bottom of the pan.

6. Take the barbecue sauce and begin to pour it over the chicken. Take a fork and spread it over the chicken. Turn chicken over and add more barbecue sauce until chicken is covered on both sides.

7. Place the chicken back into the oven for 20 more minutes uncovered until the barbecue sauce has adhered to the chicken. Remove it from the oven.

Cream of Chicken Gravy with Baked Chicken

> 1 whole chicken cut up, washed
> 4 tbsp of Old Bay seasoning
> 4 tbsp of soul food seasoning
> 2 cans of cream of chicken soup
> 2 cups of water
> Foil

8 people   50"   Easy

1. Preheat the oven to 350 degrees.

2. Place the chicken in an oven safe pan. Season the chicken with Old Bay and soul food seasoning on both sides of the chicken.

3. Place a ½ cup of water in the bottom of the pan to prevent the chicken from sticking to the pan.

4. Place the chicken in the oven and cover with foil. Cook for 45 minutes or until the chicken begins to fall off the bone.

5. Take the chicken out the oven to check for doneness by cutting chicken to look inside of it.

6. Open two cans of cream of chicken soup and place in a bowl. Take 1 ½ cups of water and mix it with the soup. Whisk the soup until it is smooth and a little runny. If it is not the right consistency, add more water and whisk together.

7. Pour the soup mixture over the chicken and make sure it is covering the chicken. Place the foil back over the top of the pan and place it back into the oven for 30 more minutes or until mixture is bubbling and slightly brown on top.

8. Remove from the oven and serve over rice.

1 Corinthians 6:17 (AMP) says, "But the one who is united and joined to the Lord is one spirit with Him."

Baked Beans

8 people   30"   Easy

---

2 large cans of Bush Molasses Baked Beans
1 ½ cups of sugar
1 stick of butter

1. In a large stock pot on medium heat, place the baked beans in a pot.

2. Add sugar and a stick of butter. Bring it to a boil.

3. Turn the heat down to medium low and cook for 25 minutes until the sauce of the beans starts thickening up from the sugar.

4. Remove from heat.

84

Mustard/Collard Greens

6 people   100"   Moderate

---

2 bunches of mustard or collards, washed and cut up
4 cups of water

10 chicken bouillon cubes
2 packs of Goya ham seasoning

3 ham hocks or smoked turkey wings
1 Power Cooker pressure

---

1. In a pressure cooker, add 3 ham hocks or smoked turkey wings and bouillon cubes with 3 cups of water.

2. Cook in the pressure cooker for 2 rounds of 50 minutes on the stew setting on the pressure cooker. Stop after these two rounds of cooking. Allow the pressure cooker to cool down by releasing the pressure on it.

3. After it has cooled down, open the lid. The ham hocks or turkey wings should be falling off the bones.

4. Add collards or mustard greens to the pressure cooker. Make sure the water is covering the greens. If not, add more water to cover them.

5. Add Goya ham seasoning packs.

6. Close the pressure cooker and close the steam releaser valve and place on another round of (2) 50-minute pressure cooking cycle.

7. After the last round cooking cycle. Serve and eat. The flavors have expanded.

Fried Cabbage

8 people   40"   Easy

---

1 medium head of cabbage, washed, cut up
3 slices of bacon, cooked

Bacon grease
3 packs of Goya Ham seasoning

3 chicken bouillon cubes, crushed
1 tbsp of soul food seasoning

---

1. In a medium stock pot, place 3 slices of bacon and cook it on low to medium heat after they are done.

2. Remove the pot from heat. Wash the cabbage to make sure they are clean.

3. Place the pot back on direct heat. Add the cabbage to the pot and place a lid tight on the pot.

4. Allow the cabbage to cook and reduce the heat down to low/medium. Stir the cabbage to make sure they are not sticking.

5. Cook the cabbage for about 25 minutes until they are your desired consistency.

6. Add 3 packs of the Goya seasoning mix to the cabbage and stir it well until thoroughly mixed.

7. 7. Add 3 chicken bouillon cubes, crush, and stir until they are well mixed.

8. Turn the cabbage down to simmer and allow it to simmer for 10 more minutes.

Ham Flavored String Beans

6 people   35"   Easy

---

3 cans of string beans, undrained

1 cup of water
3 chicken bouillon cubes

2 packs of Goya ham seasoning mix

---

1. In a medium stock pot on medium heat, add the 3 cans of string beans, undrained, 1 cup of water, and 3 chicken bouillon cubes.

2. Cook on medium heat and bring to a boil.

3. Cook for 25 minutes until the water starts receding on the green beans.

4. Add 2 packs of Goya seasoning to beans and stir until it is dissolved.

5. Cook again for 10 more minutes until almost all the water is gone from the beans.

6. Remove from heat.

Sauté Zucchini

6 people   35"   Easy

---

4 large zucchinis washed, cut into small pieces
1 tbsp of soul food seaso-ning
1 tbsp of Old Bay seaso-ning
2 packs of Goya Ham seasoning
½ tbsp of vegetable oil

---

1. In a large skillet, add oil and allow the skillet to heat up.

2. Add zucchini to the pan and stir them around in the skillet. Allow them to brown on both sides.

3. Place the lid on the skillet and allow the steam to finish cooking them.

4. Add Old Bay seasoning and soul food seasoning. Stir them until blended.

5. Add packs of Goya ham seasoning to the zucchini and stir them together.

6. Cook for 5 more minutes. Then remove the lid and remove from heat.

Baby Lima Beans with Sausages

> 1 pkg of frozen baby lima beans
> 2 or 3 ham hocks or smoked turkey wings
> 1 link of sausage, cut into small pieces
> 2 1/2 cups of water
> 2 tbsp of soul food seasoning
> 2 tbsp of Old Bay seasoning
> 5 chicken bouillon cubes
> 2 packs of Goya ham seasoning
> 1 Power Cooker pressure cooker

6 - 8 people   80"   Moderate

1. In the pressure cooker, add 2 1/2 cups of water.

2. Add the ham hocks or smoked turkey wings.

3. Add bouillon cubes, soul food and Old Bay seasoning.

4. Close the lid of the pressure cooker and close the release valve. Put on (2) 50 minutes rounds of the stew setting on the pressure cooker.

5. Open the release valve and allow the steam to escape. Now open the lid and place the baby Lima beans in the pot.

6. Add 2 packs of Goya ham flavoring and sausages to the pot.

7. Put the lid back onto the pot and cook on the stew setting for another 50 minutes.

8. After it cooks for 50 minutes, allow it to stop. Release the valve for the steam to escape and open the top.

9. Check the desired consistency of the beans and sausages. Serve on top of rice or alone.

Psalm 34:8 (AMP) says, "O taste and see that the LORD (our God) is good: He blessed (fortunate, prosperous, and favored by God) is the man who takes refuge in Him."

Baked Turkey Wings

7 people   60"   Easy

2 lb. of turkey wings cut up, washed
2 ½ cups of water
2 tbsp of Old Bay seasoning
2 tbsp of soul food seasoning
1 stick of butter or margarine

2 cans cream of chicken/mushroom soup
2 cups of water with soup
5 chicken bouillon cubes
Foil

1. Preheat oven to 350 degrees.

2. In a tin pan or oven safe pan, lay turkey wings in the bottom of the pan.

3. Season the turkey wings on both sides with Old Bay seasoning and soul food seasoning.

4. Cut the stick of butter into pieces and lay it on top of the turkey wings.

5. Add enough water to cover the turkey wings. Add bouillon cubes. Cover the pan with foil and place it in the oven.

6. Cook for 50 minutes or until meat is falling off the bones. Remove foil.

7. Mix the soup in a bowl and add 2 cups of water to get the soup smooth and flowing. Pour soup into the turkey wings.

8. Cover with foil and place back into the oven to cook for 20 to 25 more minutes until the soup is bubbling on top.

9. Remove the turkey wings from the oven and let it cool.

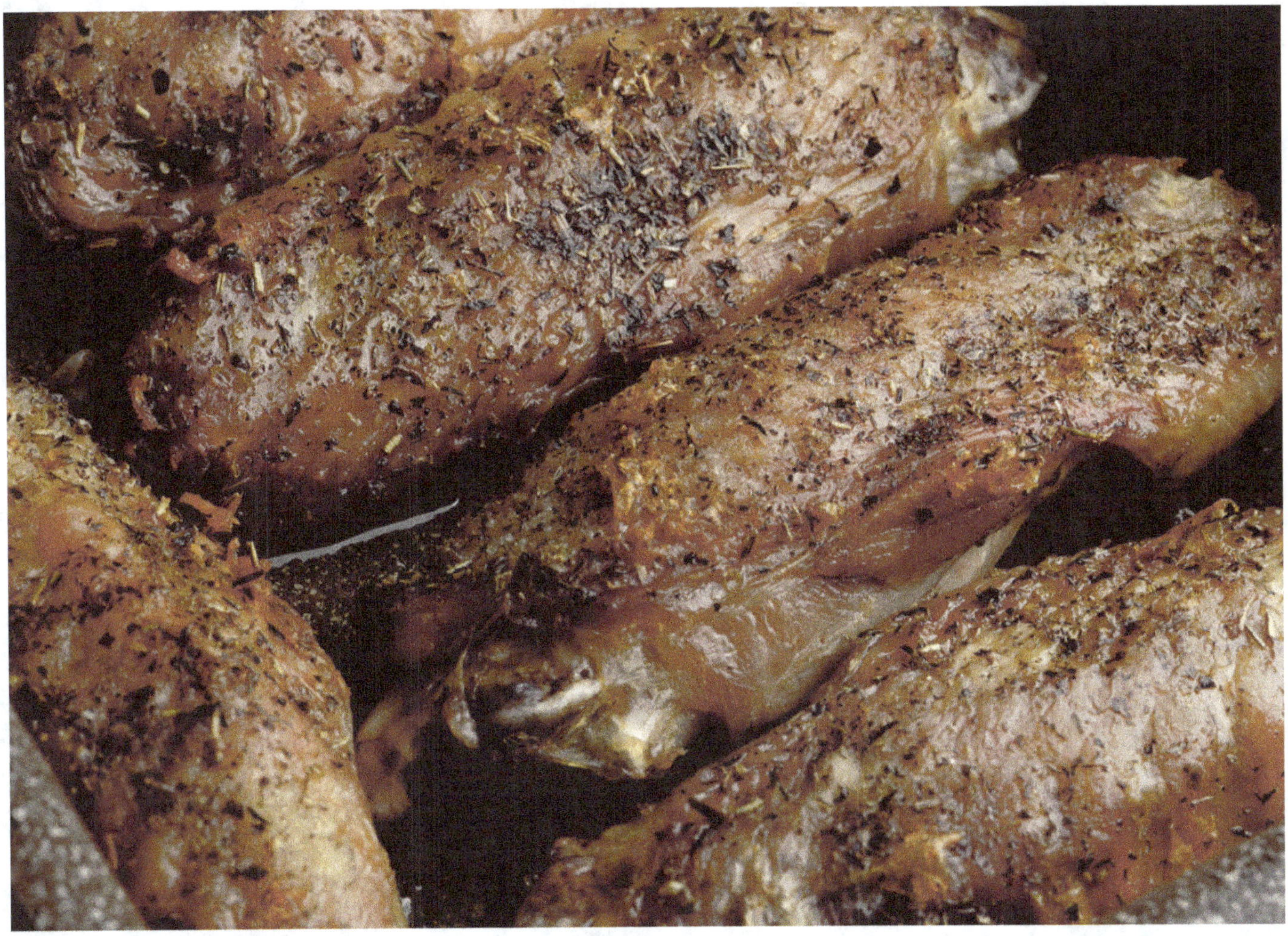

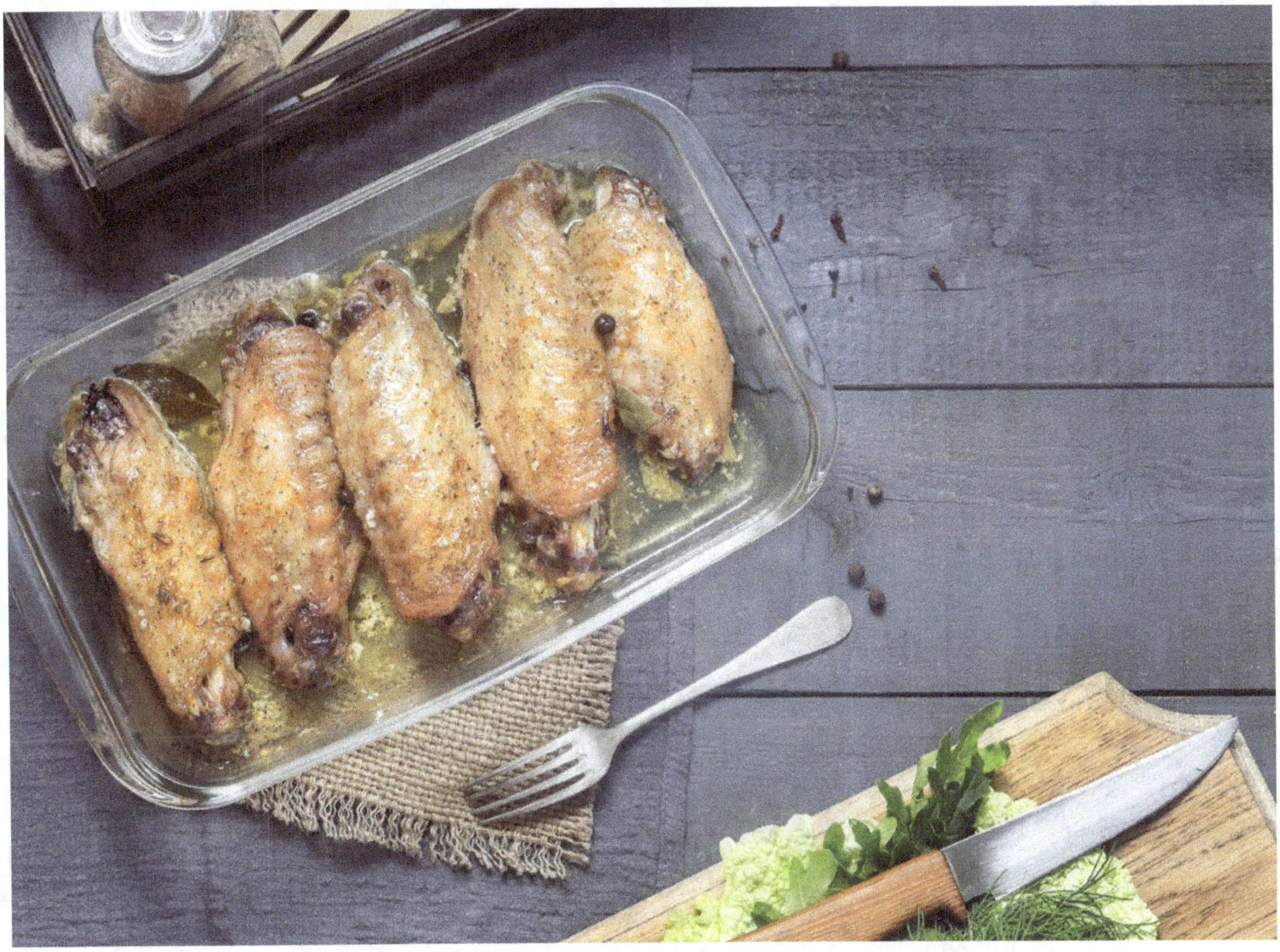

Stewed Turkey Necks

Psalm 27:1 (AMP) says, "THE LORD is my light and my salvation---Whom shall, I fear? The LORD is the refuge and fortress of my life---Whom shall I dread?"

6 people

50"

Easy

---

1 lb. of turkey necks, washed
2 celery stalks, cut up into pieces

6 chicken bouillon cubes
1 tbsp of Old Bay seasoning
1 tbsp of soul food seasoning

1 pkg of egg noodles
2 ½ cups of water

---

1. In a Power Cooker pressure cooker, place 2 ½ cups of water in the pot.

2. Add the celery, Old Bay seasoning, soul food seasonings, bouillon cubes, and turkey necks.

3. Place the lid on the pot and start a cycle of cooking on the stew setting for 50 minutes.

4. After it cooks for 50 minutes, release the steam valve and allow the steam to escape.

5. Open the lid and check the doneness of the turkey necks.

6. Put ¾ bag of egg noodles in the pot. Make sure they are covered in water. If not, add a little more water to the pot.

7. Put the lid back on the pot and start another cycle of 50 minutes on the stew setting.

8. After it finishes the cycle, the noodles will be tender and have the flavor of the turkey wings. Enjoy.

50 Weight Brown Gravy

Psalm 37:1 (AMP) says, "DO NOT worry because of evildoers, Nor be envious toward wrongdoers;"

 8 people    30"    Easy

½ tbsp of vegetable oil
4 tbsp of flour

3 cups of water
4 chicken bouillon cubes

Salt and pepper to taste

1. In a medium skillet on medium heat, add oil.

2. Heat oil, then add flour.

3. Stir flour, then brown the flour to the desired color.

4. Add 3 cups of water, bouillon cubes, salt and pepper. Allow the gravy to start boiling.

5. Turn the stove down to low heat and stir the gravy mixture to smooth it out so it can cook without lumps in it.

6. Turn the heat to simmer and simmer it for 20 minutes until the excess water is removed and the gravy is thickened as you desire.

Giblet Gravy (dressing)

Ephesians 3:20-21 (AMP) says, "Now to Him who is able to (carry out His purpose and) do superabundantly more than all that we dare ask or think (infinitely beyond our greatest prayers, hopes, or dreams), according to His power that is at work with us,   21. To Him be the glory in the church and in Christ Jesus throughout all generations forever and ever. Amen.

| 6 people | 30" | Easy |

2 cups of turkey stock, hen stock, or chicken broth

3 eggs boiled and peeled, cut up
3 tbsp of cornstarch

(add 1 tbsp to make a paste)

1. In a medium stock pot, bring the turkey stock to a boil on medium heat.

2. Add the cut up egg into the broth and cook for 1 minute.

3. Add cornstarch paste to the stock, stirring as you mix it together.

4. Cook on medium heat for 5 minutes or until the stock thickens as desired.

5. Cook 5 more minutes and remove from heat.

Buttermilk Cornbread

Luke 6:28 (AMP) says, "Bless and show kindness to those who curse you, pray for those who mistreat you."

5 people | 30" | Easy

½ cup of regular cornmeal
1/4 cup of plain flour
½ tsp of sugar
1 pinch salt

1 pinch of baking soda
1 tsp of baking powder
¼ cup of vegetable oil
1 egg

½ cup of buttermilk
2 tbsp of vegetable oil
(grease pan)

1. Preheat the oven to 425 degrees.

2. In a bowl, add everything together and mix thoroughly until well blended.

3. The bread batter should not be runny but formed and pourable. If it is a little runny, add 1 tbsp meal to the mixture and blend again.

4. Grease an oven safe pan with vegetable oil.

Pour it into a cornbread batter and shake the pan to smooth.

5. Place it into a hot oven and cook it for 8 to 10 minutes.

6. Check to make sure it is browning and not burning. If it is brown, remove it from the oven and let it stand.

Hushpuppy Sweet Cornbread

¾ cup of the house of Autry hush puppy mix
1 egg
½ cup of milk or water
2 tbsp of vegetable oil
2 tbsp of sugar

6 people   25"   Easy

Luke 6:31 (AMP) says, "Treat others the same way you want them to treat you."

1. Preheat the oven to 425 degrees.

2. Grease an oven safe pan with ½ of vegetable oil.

3. Add hush puppy mix, egg, milk, ½ oil, and sugar.

4. Mix it well together and pour it into the pan.

5. Cook for 8 to 10 minutes until it's golden brown and then cool.

6. Cut the desired size and eat.

Jiffy Cornbread Mix

🍴 6 people   🕐 30"   👨‍🍳 Easy

1 box of Jiffy Corn bread mix, make as directed.
¼ cup of sour cream
3 tbsp of sugar.
Cooking spray.

1. Preheat the oven to 425 degrees.

2. Spray an oven safe pan with cooking spray.

3. Mix the jiffy mix as directed on the box.

4. Add sour cream and sugar to the mix and mix until well blended.

5. Pour mix into a pan and place in the oven.

6. Cook for 8 to 10 minutes or until brown on the top.

7. Remove from the oven and let it sit. Enjoy.

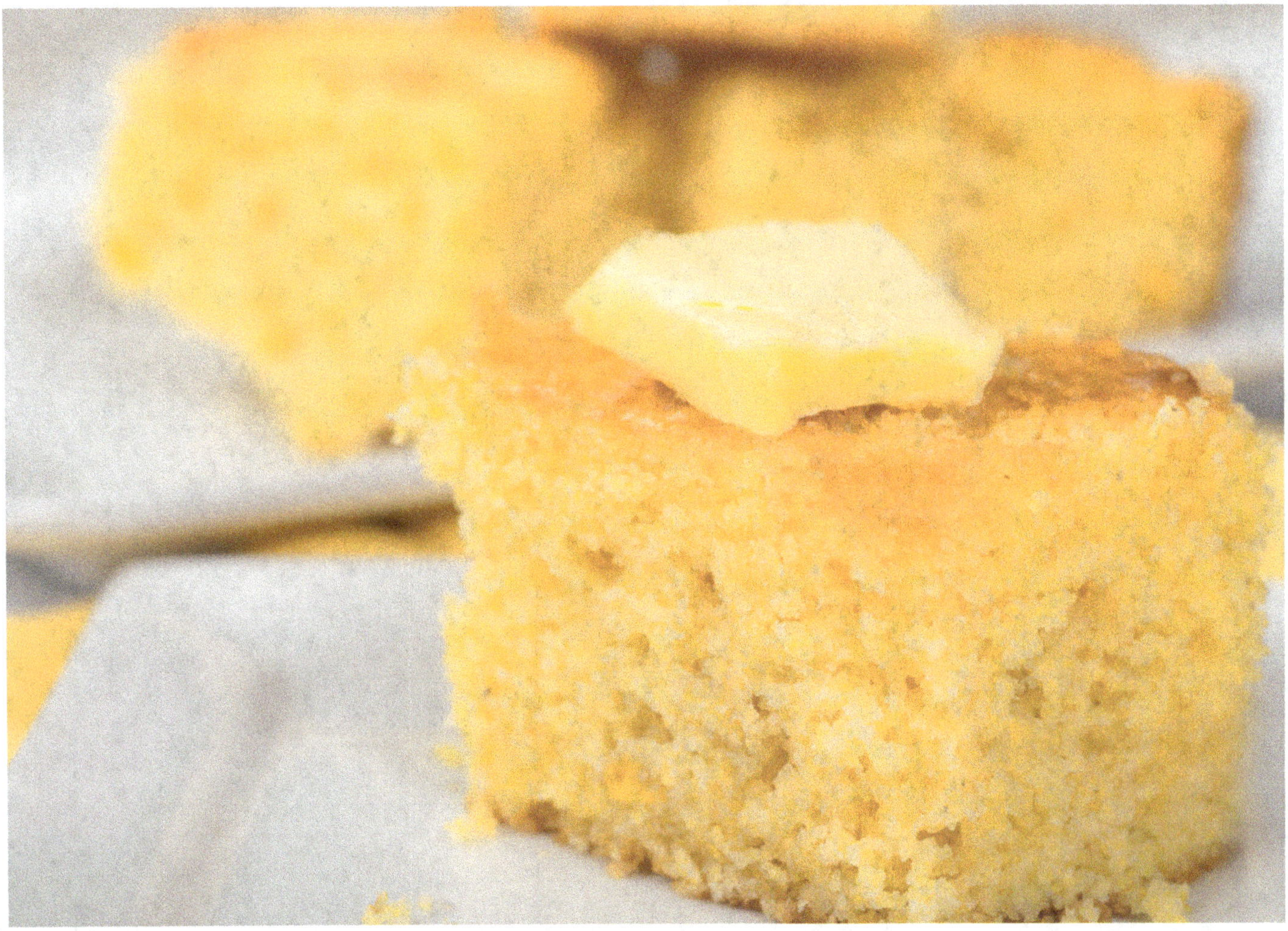

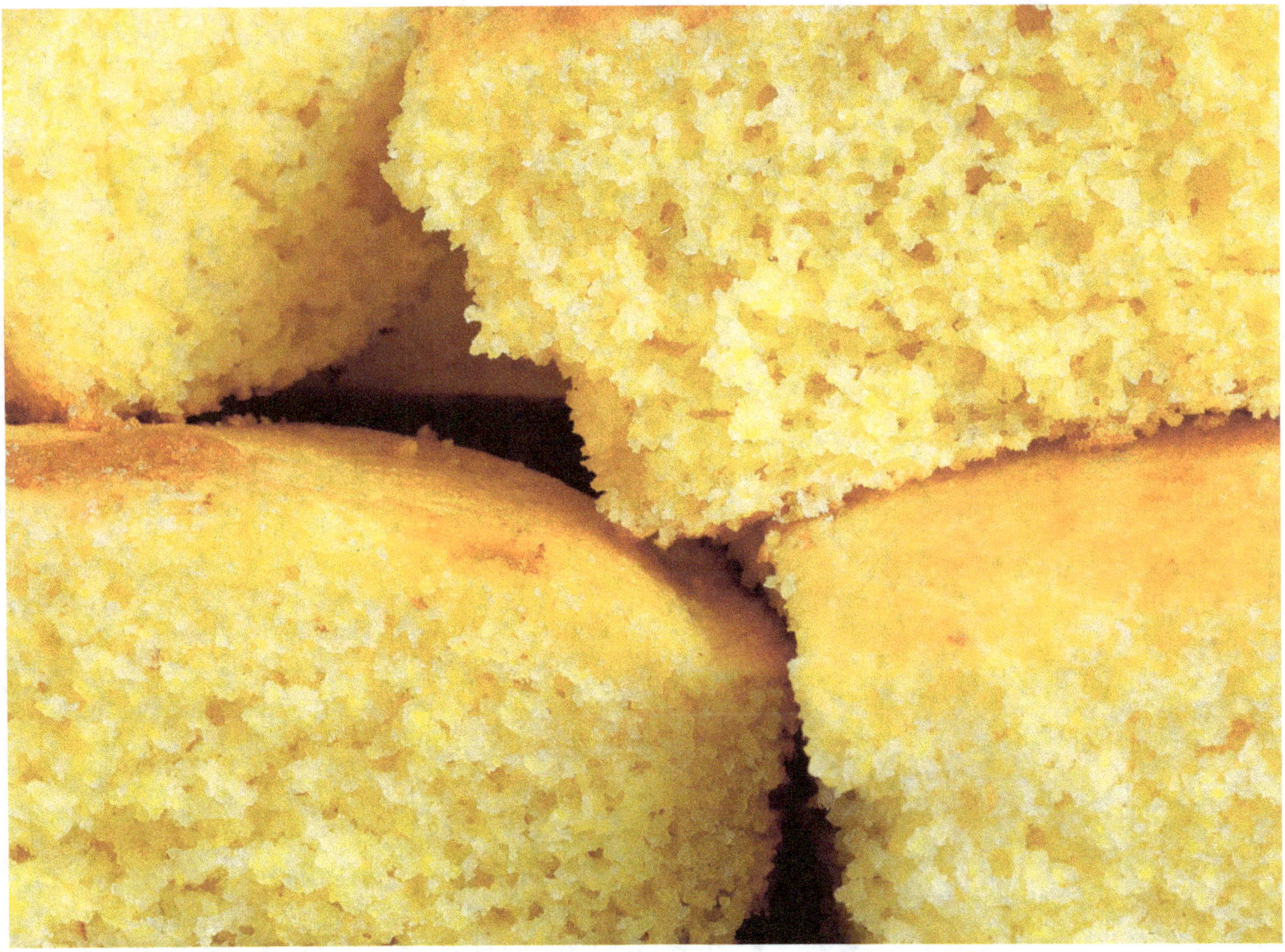

Lady Fingers

10 - 12 people   45"   Moderate

Lady fingers
2 sticks of butter, unsalted
1 cup of vegetable oil
1 cup of regular sugar
1 cup confectioners' sugar,
sifted
2 large eggs
1 tsp of vanilla
½ tsp of almond extract
4 cups of all-purpose flour
1 tsp of baking soda
1 tsp of salt
2 cups of pecans, chopped
½ cup of confectioners' sugar
for garnish

1. Preheat the oven to 350 degrees.

2. In a large bowl, cream together butter, vegetable oil, sugar, and confectioners' sugar until smooth.

3. Beat in eggs one at a time, then stir in vanilla.

4. Combine flour, baking soda, and salt. Stir into cream mixture.

5. Mix in pecans.

6. Roll dough into 1-inch balls and flatten like fingers.

7. Roll each finger in the remaining sugar.

8. Place cookies 2 inches apart on an ungreased cookie sheet.

9. Bake for 10 to 12 minutes in the oven or until the edges are golden brown.

10. Remove from the cookie sheet to cool, then dip in the remaining confectioners' sugar. Enjoy.

Soft Peanut Butter Cookies

12 people	40"	Easy

1 cup of peanut butter
1 cup of brown sugar
1 cup of sugar
1 cup of butter

2 eggs
1 tsp of baking soda
1 tsp of baking powder
1 tsp of vanilla extract

2 ½ cups of plain flour
Mixer

1. Preheat the oven to 350 degrees.

2. Cream butter, peanut butter, and both sugars together.

3. Add eggs one at a time, beating well.

4. Add baking soda, powder, and vanilla. Stir in the flour.

5. Roll into balls.

6. Use a fork to put a criss cross on the top of the cookies.

7. Bake for 20 minutes or until done.

Pecan Pie Muffins

Romans 11:29 (AMP) says, "For the gifts and the calling of God are irrevocable (for He does not withdraw what He has given, nor does He change His mind about those to whom He gives His grace or to whom He sends His call)."

12 people   35"   Easy

1 cup of packed light brown sugar
½ cup of all-purpose

flour
2 cups of chopped pecans

2/3 cup of softened butter
2 eggs beaten

1. Preheat oven to 350 degrees.

2. Grease the muffin tin or place muffin liners in the tin.

3. In a medium bowl, stir together brown sugar, flour, and pecans.

4. In a separate bowl, beat butter and eggs together.

5. Stir in dry ingredients just until combined.

6. Spoon batter into muffin cups about 2/3 full.

7. Bake for 15 to 17 minutes for muffins.

8. Allow the muffins to cool and pop them out of the muffin tin.

9. Let cool. Enjoy.

Butterfinger Cheesecake

1 Corinthians 9:14 (AMP) says, "So also (on the same principle) the Lord directed those who preach the gospel to get their living from the gospel."

6 - 8 people | 30" | Easy

1 pkg of butterfingers candy broken into small pieces

1 24.3 oz tub of Philadelphia No bake Original Cheesecake filling

1 graham cracker crust

1. Put butterfingers in a blender and chop them into small pieces. Set it aside.

2. Pour plain cream cheese inside a bowl and mix the butter finger candy with it until it is well blended.

3. Pour into graham cracker crust and put into the refrigerator for 1 hour to set.

4. Cut and then eat.

Pecan Pie

1 ½ tbsp of cornstarch
2/3 cup of sugar
1/3 cup of butter or margarine
1 cup of white corn syrup
½ tsp of salt
3 eggs
1 cup of pecan halves or broken
2 pie shells, thawed

6 people   60"   Moderate

Judges 6:12 (AMP) says, "And the angel of the LORD appeared to him and said to him, "The LORD is with you, O brave man."

1. Preheat the oven to 375 degrees.

2. In a bowl, add all ingredients except pecans.

3. Mix with a wire whisk or hand mixer.

4. Stir in pecans.

5. Pour into the pie shells.

6. Put into a hot oven and cook for 40 to 50 minutes or until the center is set. You can test it by placing a toothpick in the center. When it comes out clean, it is done. If it comes out with pie on it, put it in the oven for 10 more minutes.

7. Let cool. Enjoy

Chewy Cake

12 people   75"   Easy

---

1 Chronicles 16:10 (AMP) says, "Glory in His holy name; Let the hearts of those who seek the LORD rejoice."

2 cups of self-rising flour
½ cup of light corn syrup
2 sticks of butter
4 eggs
½ dark brown sugar, packed

2 tsp of vanilla
1 ½ cups of chopped pecans
12-16 pecans (top of the chewy cake)

1. Preheat oven to 350 degrees.

2. Melt butter in a small pot on medium heat.

3. Take off the heat and let it cool.

4. Stir in sugar and vanilla. Mix well until smooth.

5. Place eggs in a separate bowl and beat well.

6. Add cool butter to the mixture along with sugar. Mix those together until smooth.

7. Add flour. Stir until it is mixed well together.

8. Stir in pecans. The mixture will be thick.

9. Pour into greased oven safe pan and spread out in a pan.

10. Garnish with pecans on top of the chewy cake.

11. Bake for 30 to 40 minutes until the toothpick comes out clean.

12. Cool. Cut into squares. Eat.

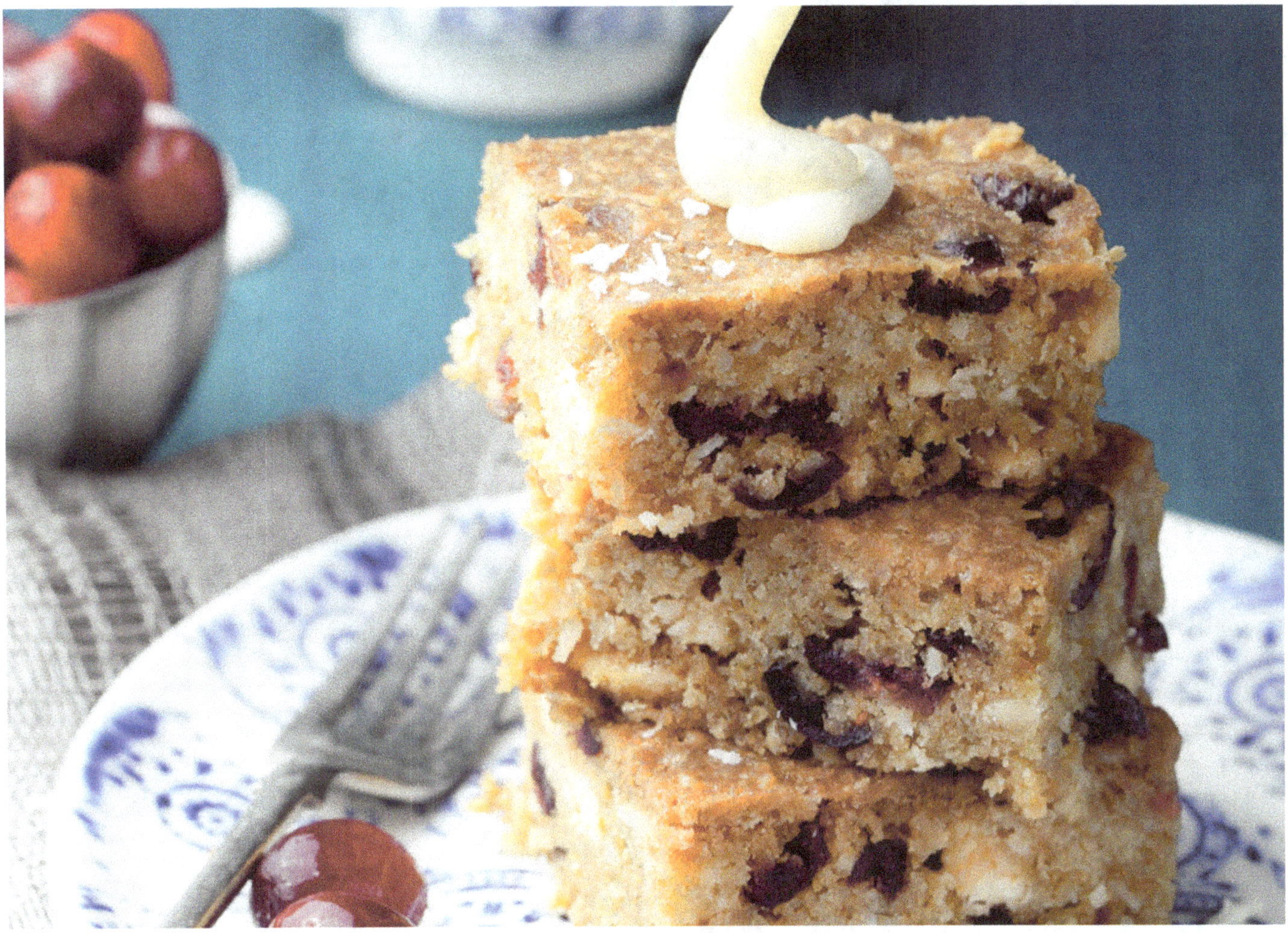

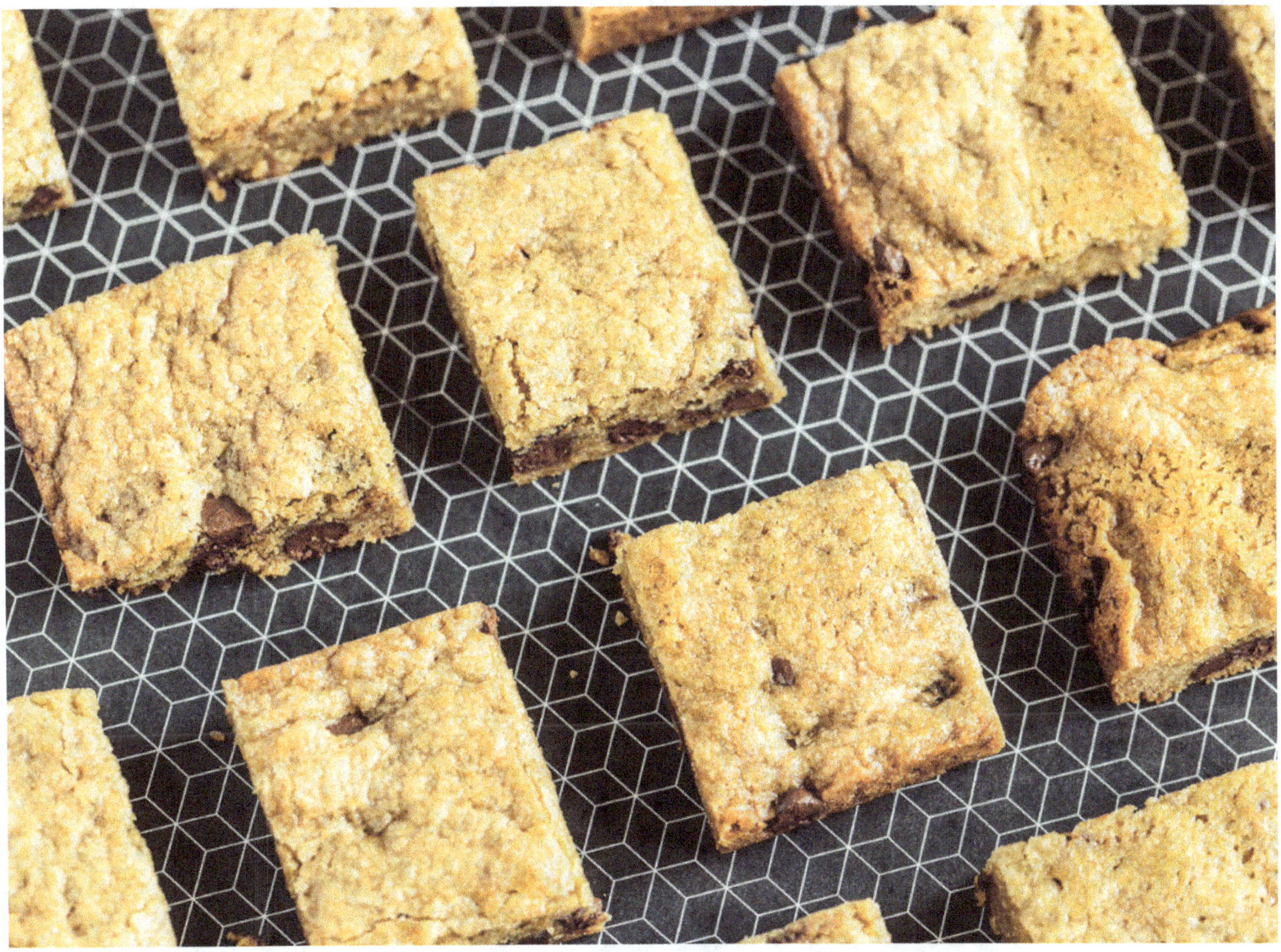

Butter Pecan Banana Cake

This cake is really good with the cream cheese icing.

10 - 15 people   79"   Moderate

---

1 pkg of Butter Recipe Golden Cake Mix
4 eggs
1 cup of mashed ripe banana (about 3 mediums)
¾ cup of vegetable oil
½ cup of sugar

¼ cup of milk
1 tsp of vanilla extract
1 tsp of lemon extract
1 cup of chopped pecans

FROSTING
1 8 oz of cream cheese

1 stick of butter or margarine, softened
1 tsp of vanilla extract
1 tsp of lemon extract
1 lb. of confectioners powdered sugar

---

1. Preheat the oven to 350 degrees.

2. Grease and flour a 10-inch Bundt or tube pan.

3. Combine cake mix, eggs, bananas, oil, sugar, milk, and vanilla extract in a large mixing bowl.

4. Beat at a low speed with an electric mixer until moistened.

5. Beat at medium speed for 2 minutes.

6. Stir in 1 cup of chopped pecans. Pour into prepared pan.

7. Bake for 50 to 60 minutes or until the toothpick inserted comes out clean.

8. Cool in pan for 25 minutes.

9. Move to a cooling rack.

FROSTING

1. Combine soft cream cheese and butter. Mix with a hand mixer.

2. Add vanilla and lemon extract. Mix well.

3. Add ½ confectioners' sugar in at a time. Mix it with the mixer until it is blended with cream cheese. Keep mixing the confectioners' sugar with the cream cheese mixture until you have used the whole bag of confectioners' sugar.

4. Place 1 cup of coarsely chopped pecans and butter in a skillet. Cook on medium heat, stirring until pecans are toasted.

5. Combine nut mixture and frosting in a bowl. Cool until it spreads consistently.

6. After the icing is cool and the cake is cool, spread the icing all over the cake.

7. Enjoy.

Key Lime Cake

10- 20 people   75"   Moderate

1 box of lemon cake mix

1 3 oz box of lime Jello   _____   temp.

1 cup of sugar   **GLAZE**   2 tbsp of lime juice

1 cup of vegetable oil   ½ cup of key lime juice   1 tsp of vanilla extract

¾ cup of orange juice   ½ cup of confectioners' sugar   1 lb. of confectioners' sugar

2 tbsp of lime juice   _____

4 eggs   **ICING**

4 drops of green food color   ½ stick of butter, room temp.

          1 pkg of cream cheese room

1. Preheat the oven to 350 degrees.

2. Grease and flour a Bundt pan.

3. In a large mixing bowl, combine lemon cake mix, gelatin, oil, lime juice, eggs, orange juice, and sugar. Stir and mix well until combined.

4. Add food color. Mix well.

5. Pour batter into Bundt pan evenly and bake for 35 to 40 minutes.

6. Test for doneness by inserting toothpick inside the cake.

7. Cool the cake in the pan for 20 minutes. Then place on cake plate.

GLAZE

1. Mix in a medium bowl, ½ cup of lime juice and confectioners' sugar.

2. Blend until mixed well together. Set it aside.

3. After the cake has cooled, take a wooden skewer and poke several holes in the top of the cake.

4. Pour glaze on the top of the cake. The glaze will soak through the top of the cake.

5. Let it settle for 20 minutes.

ICING

1. In a medium bowl, mix the cream cheese and butter together until mixed well.

2. Add vanilla extract and lime juice. Mix these into the cream cheese mixture until combined.

3. Add confectioners' sugar to the mix, at least ½ cup at a time, until all the sugar has been combined.

4. Set it aside. Frost the cake once the glaze has settled. Enjoy.

Old Fashioned Jelly Cake

Psalm 138:8 (AMP) says, "The LORD will accomplish that which concerns me; Your (unwavering lovingkindness, O LORD, endures forever---Do not abandon the works of Your own hands."

10-20 people	70"	Easy

1 box of butter golden cake mix
3 large eggs

¾ cup of water
7 tbsp of butter or margarine, melted.

1 18 oz jar of Smucker's Apple Jelly

1. Preheat oven to 350 degrees.

2. In a large bowl, add cake mix, eggs, water, and melted butter. Mix until well combined.

3. Spray a Bundt pan with cooking spray.

4. Pour batter into Bundt pan, making sure it pours even.

5. Place cake batter in a hot oven and cook for 33 to 36 minutes or until the cake is brown. To check for doneness, insert a toothpick inside of the cake. If it is clean, it is done.

6. Place on a wire rack to cool for 15 minutes.

7. Place the cake on a cake plate.

8. Open the jelly and place it in the microwave at 1-minute intervals to get it pliable enough to spread on the cake.

9. Spread jelly on the cake and let it sit for 20 minutes to cool. Enjoy.

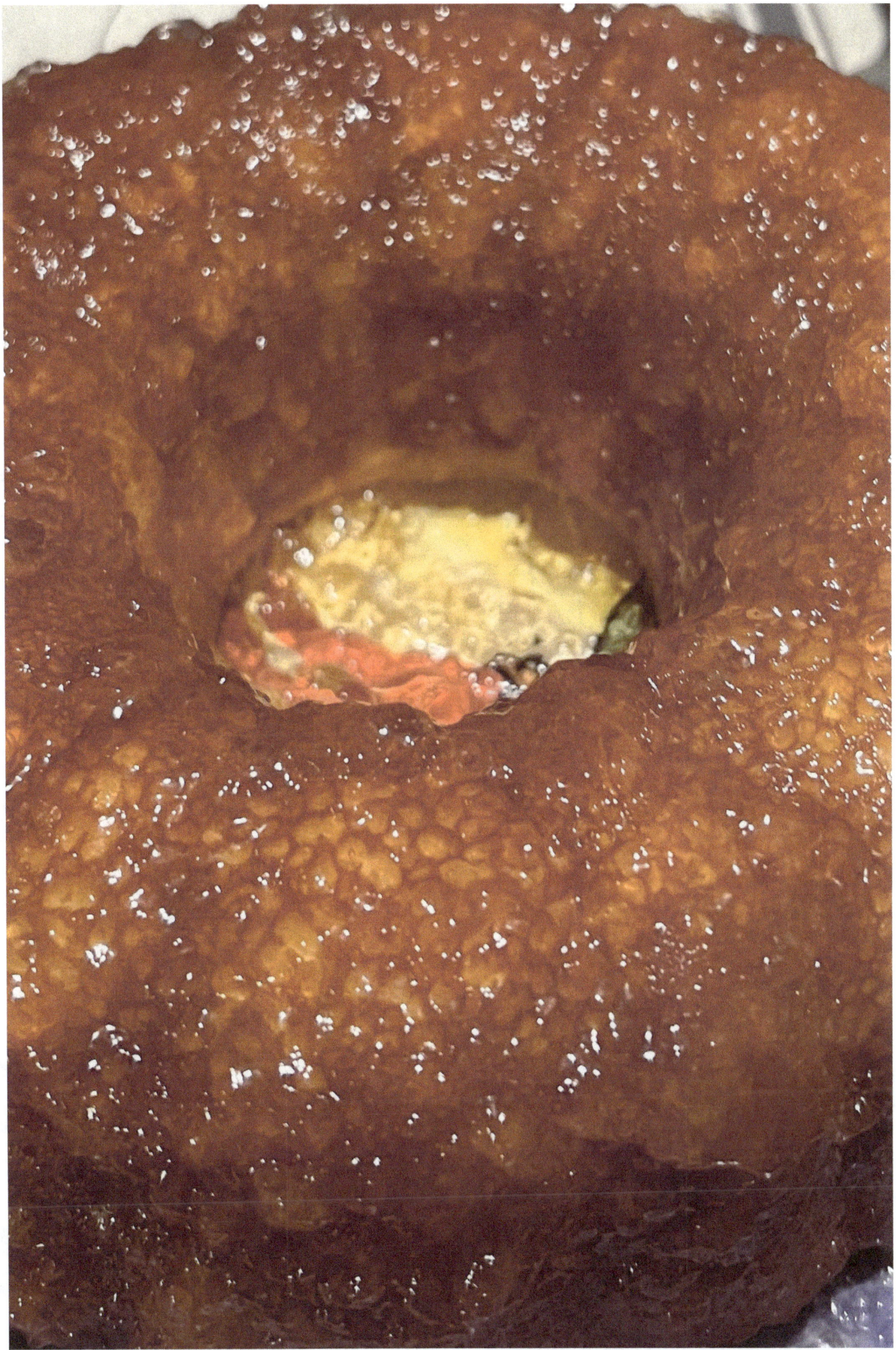

Blueberry/Blackberry Doobie

Proverbs 16:7 (AMP) says, "When a man's ways please the LORD, He makes even his enemies to be at peace with him."

6 people   40"   Easy

1 ¼ cups of sugar   2 cups of frozen berries   ½ cup of butter
1 cup of milk   1 cup of self-rising flour

1. Preheat the oven to 350 degrees.

2. Mix together sugar, flour, and milk until blended well together.

3. Whisk in melted butter.

4. Pour batter into a lightly greased glass oven safe pan.

5. Sprinkle blackberries or blueberries and the remaining sugar evenly over the batter.

6. Bake doobie for 1 hour or until the crust is golden brown and bubbly.

7. Serve with Ice cream. Enjoy.

Congealed Salad

2 3 oz pkg of cherry Jello
2 cups of boiling water
1 2 oz can of crushed pineapple, drained
1 can of strawberries, drained
1 can of cherry pie filling
1 cup of chopped nuts
1 8 oz pkg of cream cheese, softened
1 8 oz of sour cream
½ cup of confectioners' sugar
1 tsp of vanilla extract

8 people   45"   Easy

Psalm 23:4 (AMP) says, "Even though I walk through the (sunless) valley of the shadow of death, I will fear no evil, for You are with me; Your rod (to protect) and Your staff (to guide), they comfort and console me."

1. Dissolve Jello in boiling water.

2. Stir in pineapple, cherry pie filling, strawberry, and nuts.

3. Chill until set.

4. Mix together cream cheese, sour cream, confectioners' sugar, and vanilla extract until blended.

5. Spread over the top of the Jello.

6. Refrigerate until set. Eat and enjoy.

Cheesy Spinach Bacon Dip

6 - 8 people   30"   Easy

1 pkg of 10 oz frozen spinach drained and thawed
1 lb. of 16 oz Velveeta, cut into small cubes
4 oz of ½ pkg of cream cheese, softened
1 can of diced tomatoes, undrained
8 slices of bacon, cooked and crumbled
1 tsp of Old Bay seasoning
1 tsp of soul food seasoning

1. Mix all ingredients together, stirring until well mixed.

2. Microwave ingredients in a microwavable bowl on high for 5 minutes or until the Velveeta is completely melted and the mixture is well blended, stirring after 3 minutes.

124

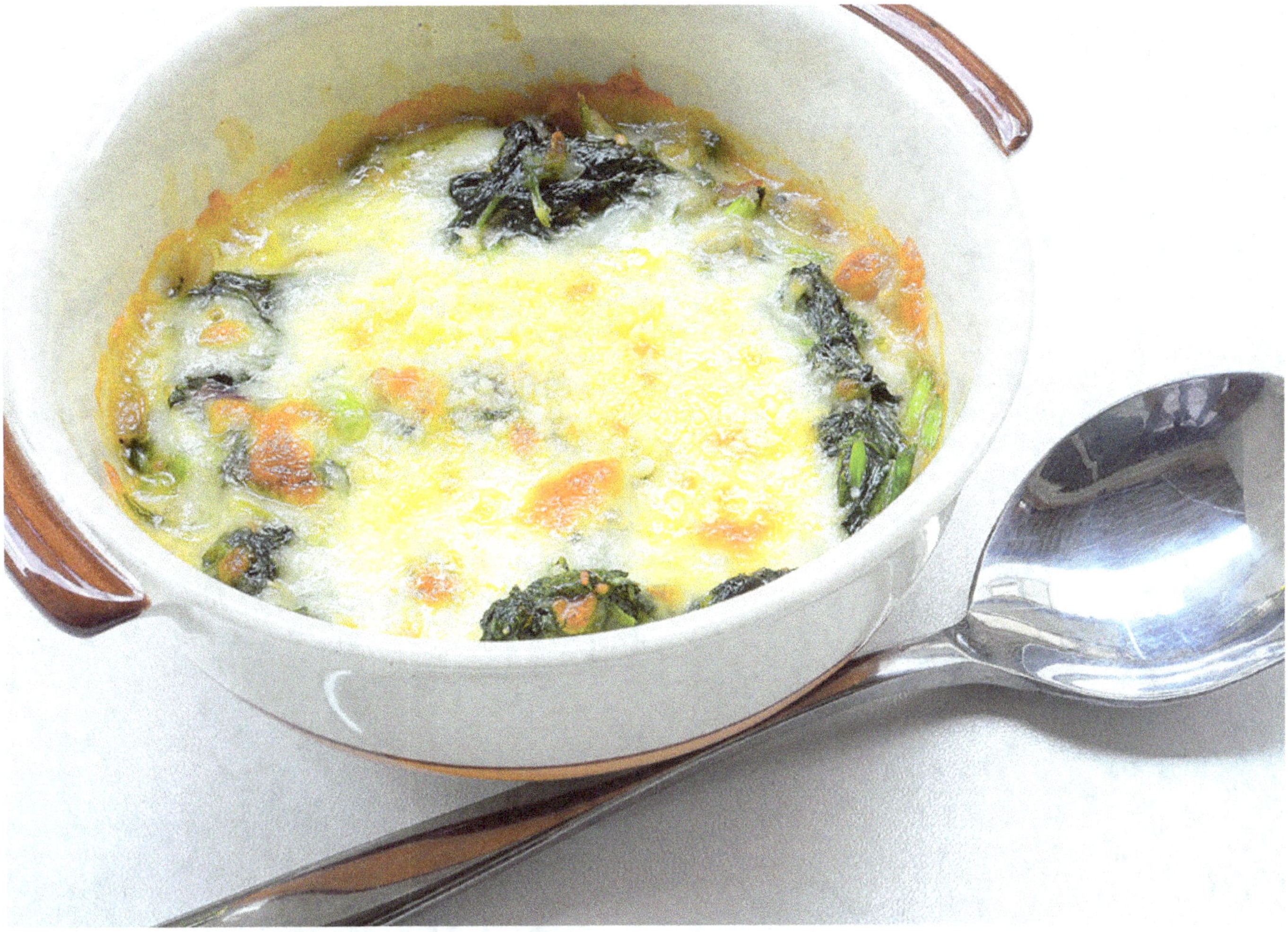

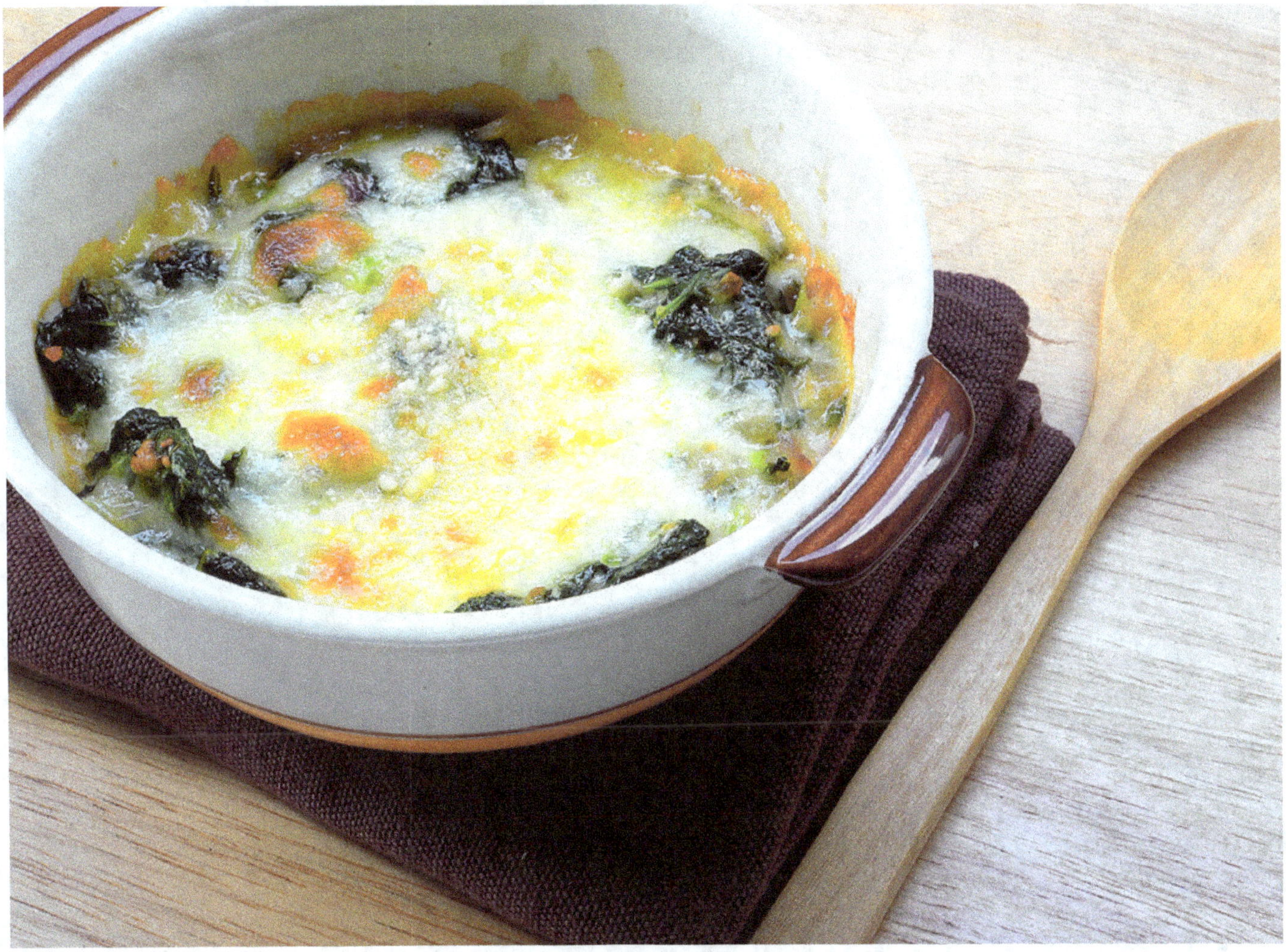

Fruit Dip #1

Dips can be served with any type of fresh fruit.
Yield 4 cups.

Psalm 119:1 (AMP) says, "HOW BLESSED and favored by God are those whose way is blameless (those with personal integrity, the upright, the guileless), Who walk in the law (and who are guided by the precepts and revealed will) of the LORD."

10 - 12 people   60"   Easy

---

1 pkg of 8 oz cream cheese, softened

½ cup of Marshmallow cream
½ cup of butter, softened

1 carton of whipped topping, thawed

---

1. In a small bowl, beat the cream cheese and butter until smooth.

2. Beat in marshmallow cream until blended with no lumps.

3. Fold in the whipped topping until blended.

4. Refrigerate if you are not going to eat immediately.

Fruit Dip #2

Yield 4 cups.

Proverbs 3:6 (AMP) says, "In all your ways know and acknowledge and recognize Him, And He will make your paths straight and smooth (removing obstacles that block your way)."

| 10- 12 people | 80" | Easy |

1 pkg of 8 oz cream chee-se, softened

1 16 oz of strawberry yo-gurt, plain

½ cup of powdered sugar
Assorted fruit.

1. In a small bowl, beat the cream chee-se until smooth.

2. Add strawberry yogurt to the mix-ture and blend until the mixture is smooth.

3. Add powdered sugar and blend until mixed well.

4. Refrigerate and let it chill for at least an hour before serving.

5. Serve with fresh fruit.

Nacho Dip

10-25 people   45"   Easy

---

2 pkg of 16oz Velveeta cheese Dip and Sauce, cut into cubes

24 oz of Pace chunky salsa
½ cup of sour cream
1 bag of Restaurant Style

Tortilla Chips
1 Reynolds slow cooker liners

---

1. Place a liner in a large crock pot on high heat.

2. Place Velveeta cheese cubes inside the crock pot and heat until melted, stirring occasionally.

3. Pour 1 jar of Pace chunky salsa into the cheese and mix well until blended.

4. Pour sour cream into the pot and stir until well blended and mixed together.

5. Turn the crockpot on warm to keep the cheese warm and flowing. Enjoy.

Beef Cheese Dip

Revelation 3:20 (AMP) says, "Behold, I stand at the door (of the church) and continually knock. If anyone hears My voice and open the door, I will come in and eat with him (restore him), and he with Me."

5 - 8 people   45"   Easy

1 lb. of Ground beef, cooked
2 lbs. of Velveeta cheese, cut into cubes

1 16 oz of mild Pace Picante sauce
1 tsp of Old Bay seasoning

1 tsp of soul food seasoning

1. Melt cheese in a crock pot.

2. Brown meat.

3. Add cheese mixture and seasoning to this mixture.

4. Add the Picante sauce.

5. Simmer for 30 minutes until fully heated.

6. Serve with chips or crackers.

Homemade Lemonade

5 lemons
1 lemon cut into slices
2 ½ cups of sugar
4 cups of water
1 lemon squeezer
1 large 3 Liter pitcher

6 - 8 people   20"   Easy

John 14:1 (AMP) says, "DO NOT let your heart be troubled (afraid, cowardly). Believe (confidently) in God and trust Him, (have faith), hold on to it, rely on it, keep going and) believe also in Me."

1. Cut lemons in half and put them on top of the lemon squeezer. Squeeze the juice out of lemons. Set it aside.

2. Take out the seeds.

3. Put sugar in the pitcher. Put the juice in the pitcher.

4. Add water until the pitcher is filled up to the fill line.

5. Take a long spoon and stir all the contents together until well blended.

6. Take slices of lemon and put inside of the pitcher.

7. Chill lemonade in the refrigerator.

Sweet Tea

6 - 10 people   20"   Easy

---

2 tea bags
4 cups of water
2 ½ cups of sugar
1 large 3-liter pitcher

Matthew 6:10 (AMP) says, "Your kingdom come, Your will be done on earth as it is in heaven."

1. Put 4 cups of water in a medium stock pot on medium heat.

2. Place the tea bags in water and bring them to a boil. When the tea starts boiling, cut it off.

3. Leave steeping for 5 minutes.

4. Place sugar in the pitcher and add tea and water. Stir until blen-

ded together until well mixed.

5. Chill tea in the refrigerator.

Homemade Strawberry Lemonade

Psalm 55:22 (AMP) says, "Cast your burden on the LORD (release it) and He will sustain and uphold you; He will never allow the righteous to be shaken (slip, fall, fail)."

10 - 20 people

25"

Easy

---

5 lemons
1 lemon sliced into slices
2 ½ cups of sugar

3 cups of water
½ strawberries or pureed strawberries

1 lemon squeezer
1 large 3-liter pitcher

---

1. Cut lemons in half and put them on top of a lemon squeezer. Squeeze juice out of lemons. Set it aside.

2. Take out seeds.

3. Put sugar in the pitcher.

4. Add lemon juice to the pitcher. Add water and fill it up to the line.

5. Take a long spoon and stir all the contents together until well mixed.

6. Pour pureed strawberries inside the pitcher and stir the contents together.

7. Add sliced lemons.

8. Chill in refrigerator. Enjoy.

Ham, Oh so good Peanuts

5- 8 people   90"   Easy

---

1 ½ lb. of raw boiling peanuts
2 pkg of Goya Seasoning

Ham flavor
4 cups of water
¼ cup of salt

6 chicken bouillon cubes, crushed
1 pressure cooker

---

1. Place peanuts, Goya seasoning, water, salt, and bouillon cubes in the pressure cooker pot.

2. Turn the pressure cooker on to the stew setting for (2) 50-minute intervals.

3. Release the pressure valve to allow the steam to escape on the last setting.

4. Check peanuts to see if they are salty enough. If they aren't, just allow the peanuts to soak in the juice for at least 30 minutes as they cool. Enjoy.

CONCLUSION

These are the recipes I have tried over the years since I have been married and I am still cooking these today. I have critiqued them the way that my husband and I like them. These are some very tasty dishes that would bring something extra to any dinner table, birthday party, Thanksgiving, or Christmas. I wanted to share these dishes that have been a blessing to my family and me with your family. The scriptures included are food for your spirit that will help you be able to not only eat natural food, but spiritual food as well. I would like to personally thank everyone who has purchased this cookbook, used these recipes for the food, and used the Word of God to empower you for greatness in God. I pray Godspeed to all who have thought it was not robbery to purchase this cookbook.

*****Thank You from the Richardson's Richard & Angela Richardson*****

ABOUT THE AUTHOR

Dr. LaRose Angela Richardson is the wife of Richard Richardson and the mother of Satara Cowan. She has one granddaughter, Allara Cowan. She has lived in Southeast Georgia all of her life. In May 2016, she graduated with a Doctor's Degree in Theology from Crossland Christian University in Orlando, Florida. She is the co-author of "It Cost Me Everything" written by Prophetess Kimberly Moses. She also has 4 other books that she has written. The first one is "Walking in Total Freedom after Healing from Deep Inner Wounds," and the second one is "Prayers that Availeth Much," and her third book is "180 days of Communing with God Daily Devotional," and her fourth book is "Part 2 180 days of Communing with God Daily Devotional." She has started a blog this year under Refiner's Fire Deliverance Ministries, which can be found at ministerrich0628.blogspot.com. Her ministry page can be found on Facebook "Refiner's Fire Deliverance Ministries, and you can go on this page weekly every Thursday for a Powerful Word from the Lord. She has a linktr.ee/AngelasDesignerCrafts where all of her latest books and ministry materials are as well. She also has a business page on Facebook: Angela's Designer Crafts. Check her out for all of your unique gift needs. She can be contacted on Facebook on her ministry page, her business page, or her personal page "Angela Richardson." You can also email her at ministerrich0628@gmail.com.

ABOUT THE AUTHOR

Dr. Richard C. Richardson is married to LaRose A. Richardson. They have been married for 13 years and counting. He received his doctor's degree in May 2016 from Crossland Christian University in Orlando, FL. He is the owner of Richard's Detailing and Richardson's Hardwood Floor Refinishing; this is his first joint venture with his wife. He loves to cook as well and has several dishes that he excels with as well. He is a member of Becoming One Outreach Ministries with Apostle Troy Williams and Pastor Carmella Williams, where He serves as the Pastor over the men's group in the church. He also is on the intercessors' team in his local church, and he serves there with his wife, LaRose. They believe that one can chase a thousand, but two can chase ten thousand. He believes in touching, agreeing, and praying the Word of God over a situation. He believes that as we pray, God will answer our prayers. He can be contacted through his email ocelotbaconz@yahoo.com; his Facebook page is Richard Richardson, also his business page Richardson's Hardwood Floor Refinishing. He can be contacted through their ministry page Refiner's Fire Deliverance Ministries on Facebook.

www.ingramcontent.com/pod-product-compliance
Lightning Source LLC
Chambersburg PA
CBHW080850120626
46546CB00008B/2763